Beyond Mayberry

LHP

Also By Thomas D. Perry

Ascent To Glory: The Genealogy of J. E. B. Stuart

The Free State of Patrick: Patrick County Virginia In The Civil War

Images of America: Patrick County Virginia

Images of America: Henry County Virginia

Then and Now: Patrick County Virginia

Notes From The Free State Of Patrick: Patrick County, Virginia, and Regional History

God's Will Be Done: The Christian Life of J. E. B. Stuart

Patrick County Oral History Project: A Guide

Upward Toil: The Lester Family of Henry County Virginia

Mount Airy, North Carolina

Martinsville, Virginia

Henry County Heritage Book Volume One

J. E. B. Stuart Birthplace

Fieldale, Virginia

"If Thee Must Fight, Fight Well." William J. Palmer and the Fight for Martinsville, April 8, 1865

The Graham Mansion: A History

Visit www.freestateofpatrick.com for more information

Beyond Mayberry

**A Memoir of Andy Griffith
and Mount Airy North Carolina
By
Thomas D. Perry**

ISBN-13: 978-1478191629

ISBN-10: 1478191627

Laurel Hill Publishing LLC
P. O. Box 11
4443 Ararat Highway
Ararat, VA 24053
www.freestateofpatrick.com
276-692-5300
freestateofpatrick@yahoo.com

Cover and title page are of Andy Griffith and his parents Carl and Geneva Nunn Griffith on June 1, 1957, Andy's 31st birthday on "Andy Griffith Day" in Mount Airy for the movie premiere of *A Face in the Crowd*.

**For my cousins,
Todd and Jonathan Perry,
and their families.**

Remembering their mother at Tharrington School with this
granite bench are Lisa, Todd, Grant, Paige, and Jonathan Perry.
The inscription states, "In Loving Memory of Gwen Perry, who
touched the lives of many children."

Reed Perry, Grant Perry and the author's mother Betty Hobbs Perry at the statue of Andy and Opie going fishing in Mount Airy, North Carolina.

"People started saying that Mayberry was based on Mount Airy…It sure sounds like it, doesn't it."
Andy Griffith, 2002

Citations for Recipients of the 2005
Presidential Medal of Freedom
Andy Samuel Griffith

Andy Griffith is one of America's best-known and most beloved entertainers. After his introduction to a national audience as a stand-up comedian on The Ed Sullivan Show in the 1950s, he went on to star in such celebrated television shows as The Andy Griffith Show and Matlock. As a legend of the stage, cinema, and television, Andy Griffith has built an enduring career and set a standard of excellence in entertainment. He is a man of humor, integrity, and compassion. The United States honors Andy Griffith for demonstrating the finest qualities of our country and for a lifetime of memorable performances that have brought joy to millions of Americans of all ages.

You can view the ceremony online at
http://www.c-spanvideo.org/program/189856-1

"Here at the White House, we get an interesting mix of visitors. Already today I've met with the Secretary of State, Secretary of Defense, and the Dalai Lama -- and the Sheriff of Mayberry. Andy Griffith first came to the people's attention with his gift for storytelling -- and his own life is a mighty fine story by itself. He started out as a high school teacher, and in his amazing career he has gained fame as an actor, and received a Grammy Award for his singing. He will always be remembered for *The Andy Griffith Show* and *Matlock*. Yet, he has also given powerful dramatic performances in such movies as 'A Face in the Crowd.'

Looking back on his Mayberry days, Andy explained the timeless appeal of the show. He said 'it was about love. Barney would set himself up for a fall, and Andy would be there to catch him.' The enduring appeal of the show has always depended -- and still does -- on the simplicity and sweetness and rectitude of the man behind the badge. TV shows come and go, but there's only one Andy Griffith. And we thank him for being such a friendly and beloved presence in our American life."

-- President George W. Bush at the White House, November 9, 2005

Russell Hiatt, who started the Mayberry effect in Mount Airy in the 1980s.

Contents

Foreword July 3, 2012   13

Chapter One Andy's Civil War   23

Chapter Two Patrick County Connections   31

Chapter Three Double Birthdays in Mount Airy   37

Chapter Four Growing up on Haymore Streets   43

Chapter Five Trombone Lessons   57

Chapter Six Beyond Mount Airy   69

Chapter Seven Can You Go Home Again   81

Chapter Eight Mayberry in Mount Airy   91

Chapter Nine Beyond Mayberry   133

Chapter Ten Mayberry on Main Street   143

Chapter Ten A Life in Pictures   153

Afterword July 4, 2012   195

Afterword July 4, 2013   209

Selected Bibliography   235

About The Author   237

Acknowledgements   241

Index   243

July 3, 2012, in Mount Airy, North Carolina

"I appreciate it and good night."

He was 86 years old on the morning of July 3, 2012. He had spent a restless night. He got up and sat in a wheelchair. Early that morning his heart stopped beating and Andy Griffith passed away. He died at his estate on Roanoke Island along Highway 64/264 about 330 miles from his birthplace in Mount Airy. We will never know what his last thoughts were, but we would like to think that it was of home, the place he made famous as Mayberry on *The Andy Griffith Show* for eight years on CBS. North Carolinian Thomas Wolfe wrote that "You Can't Go Home Again," but Andy Griffith never left Mount Airy and he carried it to the world.

When I think of *The Andy Griffith Show*, I think of peanut butter. As a teenager getting off the bus from high school around 4 p.m. in Ararat, Virginia, before I could drive and get a "real job" in Mount Airy, after petting Susie, my collie dog, the first thing I went for was a peanut butter sandwich with or without jelly whether it was grape, strawberry, or even apple. Relaxing on the couch with a big glass of my mother's powerhouse sweet tea and the above-mentioned sandwich sometimes involved watching an episode of *The Wild Wild West* or *Gomer Pyle USMC* from WFMY channel 2 out of Greensboro delivered on the antenna high above my parent's home. This was in the days before cable and satellite.

A couple of hours of alone time might include basketball with the neighbors or mowing the grass. Every afternoon included at least one half hour of *The Andy Griffith Show* with Andy, Opie, and especially Barney usually between five and six. My personal opinion is that there was nothing funnier on television in my youth than Don Knotts playing the clown to Andy Griffith's straight man. I always thought Andy Griffith looked bored after Knotts left the show to make movies.

My mother arrived home from her thirty-eight years shipping golf shirts for Quality Mills, later Cross Creek Apparel, to make dinner for me and my father, who tried to play golf every afternoon after a day either teaching or being Principal at Red Bank, then Blue Ridge Elementary School. This couple, like several others I came to know later, met while the man was in the

U. S. Army stationed at Fort Gordon, just outside my mother's hometown of Augusta, Georgia. They met at a barbeque place in the downtown of the Peach State's Garden City. My father's family came from a little town about an hour west of Chattanooga, Tennessee, where my father was born at the end of 1931. The Perrys, two sets of them Uncle John and his nephew another Erie, my grandfather, the heads of the two families came to Mount Airy, North Carolina in the 1940s.

I was born in the Northern Hospital of Surry County in Mount Airy, North Carolina, just down the hill and within sight of the home where Andy Griffith spent most of his time growing up and where he returned in 2002 to spend the night before U. S. Highway 52 became The Andy Griffith Parkway. I came into the world the same year that Andy Griffith became Sheriff Andy Taylor on October 3, 1960, exactly one month and one day before I was born on November 4.

I grew up in Patrick County, Virginia, where Andy's mother Geneva Nunn Griffith grew up near the waters of the Dan River, a few miles from the waters of the Ararat River, where I grew up. Patrick County never felt like home. Mount Airy felt

more like home, but it was not where I grew up. Mount Airy was

home to me mainly because my father spent his later teen there and

my grandparents lived there after moving from Chattanooga,

Tennessee, in the late 1940s.

Haymore Baptist Church was the reason to go to Mount

Airy every Sunday and sometimes on Wednesdays to be an RA, a

Royal Ambassador, the program for children in what was really the

Second Baptist Church, but named for a pastor with the name of

Haymore. Andy Griffith attended Haymore Baptist Church and

grew up on Haymore Street, just a few blocks south.

Andy Griffith made his way to the Grace Moravian Church

when the pastor there encouraged his music and comedic talents. I

made my way to my paternal grandparent's apartment on West

Pine Street in the Graves House after Sunday School avoiding the

regular 11 a. m. service. Looking back on it, I loved Sunday

School because it was all about history.

History is what it is all about for me and this little book is

part memoir, my history, and part biography, Andy Griffith's history, and the town we both share along the Virginia/North Carolina border. Although I never met him, like many I feel he has been part of my life forever.

Not only did I share Haymore Baptist on Rockford Street with Andy Griffith, I realized that we were both only children, who discovered music as a way to escape the doldrums and loneliness of childhood. I spent one hot summer working in a tobacco field to buy in Mount Airy for a $100 Yamaha guitar from Easter Brother's Music Shop and found a teacher at church, but unlike Andy, who swept out buildings for $6 a week to purchase a trombone, I did not have to leave Haymore and go across town to find a teacher. I found church member Sam Dobyns, who spent many hours teaching me chords to 1974 albums such as Ringo Starr's *Ringo* and Paul McCartney's *Band on the Run*.

The idea to write this book came to me one rainy day in April 2012 while I was recovering from prostate cancer surgery. The word cancer in the vocabulary of a 51-year-old man, humbled by the after effects, gives one time to pause and think about his life. My mind wandered to the happy days I spent with my grandparents in their apartment just a few houses down from the Mount Airy Library in Kochtitzky House.

All of that came full circle on July 3, 2012, when word reached Mount Airy that Andy Griffith died early that morning on Roanoke Island on the Atlantic Coast, where he lived most of his adult life. Soon news came that the most famous man from the town at the foot of the Blue Ridge Mountains would remain along the coast instead of coming home to rest in Grace Moravian Church Cemetery as many suspected when Andy rejoined the church several years previous. The idea of Graceland and Grace Moravian was not to be. North Carolinian Thomas Wolfe was right when he penned *You Can't Go Home Again* and so it was for Andy Samuel Griffith, but Griffith did not necessarily have to come home as he took home with him and put his hometown on the map and on television.

For many of his fans Andy Griffith was the ultimate television father. In real life, he admitted he was not nearly as good a father as Andy Taylor, but for fathers and sons you could not ask for a better relationship than Andy and Opie Taylor. It was my father's family that brought me to Mount Airy and so the only encounter between the "two legends" follows.

In 1966 before I started school, my father, Erie Meredith Perry stood in line at the Hospital Pharmacy across Rockford Street from the Northern Hospital of Surry County he recounted to me on July 3, 2012. The Pharmacist Bob Smith looked up and said, "Well, Hello Andy." My father realized that Andy Griffith was standing in line with him and neither "legend in their own time or minds" spoke to each other. I never knew my father to be without words in the fifty plus years I have known him, but apparently, Andy was not in a speaking mood. He was there on personal business specifically to have his mother's medicine billed to him as it was recounted to me under a tent at Pilot Mountain's Mayfest just a few days later by the then owner of the Hospital Pharmacy. It was probably this sort of thing that led Andy Griffith to move his parent's Carl and Geneva Nunn Griffith to California in 1966 so they could be closer to their only son.

My father grew up a poor boy in Mount Airy. I found many parallels in the lives of the two men who met across the street from where I was born. After years of speaking on J. E. B. Stuart all over the country, whenever I said I was from Mount Airy almost always the next thing people said related to Andy Griffith or Mayberry.

On the afternoon of July 3 as Andy Griffith was laid to rest on the coast, the clouds opened up on Mount Airy as if the sky was crying over the loss of its favorite son. I found myself watching the television coverage and later episodes on WFMY of *The Andy Griffith Show*, where I first watched Jim West, Gomer Pyle and Andy Taylor.

I found myself strangely emotional about it. Earlier in the day, I went to tell my father that Andy Griffith was dead. He did not know it as he was lost in an old movie on Turner Classic Movies, a love of the movies he passed on to his only son. We spoke a few minutes about Andy as my father, who was half through his eightieth year on the day Griffith died, went to the same high school, but did not know him. They did have much in common though especially growing up in Mount Airy and I always think of them together when I ponder the subject.

As a boy I remember walking up Pine Street to Main Street in Mount Airy and having a hot dog at the Snappy Lunch with my grandmother or watching my grandfather get his hair cut next door in the City Barber Shop, now Floyd's City Barber Shop.

Later, I took a class in Appalachian Studies at Virginia Tech. The professor could not say enough bad things about Andy Griffith. Her thesis was that every known stereotype to make Southerners look stupid was on display in the show and that he was cutting them with such a sharp knife they did not even feel it. I wonder what she would think of the plethora of tourists, who visit every year for Mayberry Days.

It is easy to criticize those who promote the idea of Mayberry, but for them it represents the wholesome, nostalgic, and sanitized feelings we hope our hometown will have. Mount Airy is trying to become Hannibal, Missouri, where Tom Sawyers and Becky Thatchers roam the street bringing the writings of Mark Twain to life. Just like Hannibal, where Huck Finn is ignored, there are only white faces in Mayberry. It is not a real place with real problems.

Sheriff Hudson Graham of Surry County once said, "We're not exactly Mayberry, but then in many ways we are. Folks come here with their problems, just as they do to Andy Griffith. Only thing, his writers are better at contriving happy endings than we can manage."

I was present when Highway 52 was named the Andy Griffith Parkway. Cagey as he was as Sheriff Taylor, Andy hinted that the town Mayberry was based on Mount Airy. He never confirmed it, but I have a theory. I imagine an actor in Hollywood in the early 1960s working with others to come up with the design for a show. The actor remembers as a young boy traveling with his father along the Blue Ridge Parkway stopping in for a bottle of pop at a place called Mayberry. Shazam!

This is my opinion and the history of the town where I was born and the story of the most famous man to come from it. Thanks Andy for the entertainment. I appreciate it and good night. For you "Constant Reader," as Stephen King might say, have a good read about Andy Griffith and Mount Airy.

Following "Stonewall" Jackson was tough on many men during the War Between the States. The only way to avoid service was death, sickness, or a wound. Andrew J. Nunn of North Carolina found himself as part of the latter as his compatriots in the 21st North Carolina Infantry Regiment moved down to the peninsula between the James and York Rivers to fight with Robert E. Lee's Army of Northern Virginia in the summer of 1862.

Nunn found himself left behind at Mount Jackson, Virginia, in the Shenandoah Valley at the beginning of June 1862. Although Mount Jackson was not named for Thomas J. Jackson, who received his famous sobriquet "Stonewall" at the Battle of First Manassas as the Southerners called it, the valley became famous for the exploits of Jackson, the former VMI Professor. The Yankees called it First Bull Run when South Carolinian General Bee told his men to "look at Jackson standing like a stonewall."

Nunn probably received a wound at the First Battle of Winchester on May 25, 1861. The regiment lost 21 killed and 60 wounded. Serving under Richard Ewell's Division in the brigade of Isaac Trimble, Nunn saw some hot action. One internet blogger described it this way. "Dawn of May 25th found Banks' forces defensively positioned on a range of protective hills just south of the town. Jackson launched assaults on both Federal flanks and immediately encountered fierce resistance. On the Confederate right, near the Front Royal road, Trimble ordered his "two Twenty Firsts" to charge a strongly positioned Union regiment. A member of the 21st North Carolina described the ensuing charge: "With a wild cheer the regiment moved swiftly towards the enemy's line behind stone walls, and was met by a most terrific fire of infantry and grape shot. The regiment moved right on to the stone wall, from which the enemy were pouring forth a perfect storm of canister and minie balls from right and left–cross-firing upon us." Despite initially wavering in the intense fire, the Carolinians regrouped and joined their brothers in the 21st Georgia in driving the Federals from the field."

Nunn possibly was one of thirteen wounded at Cross Keys and Port Republic culminating Jackson's Valley Campaign, one of the most famous military maneuvers in history. Andy Nunn recovered from his wound to fight on.

He had brothers in the war. Private Jefferson Nunn died at age 24 on September 25, 1861, at Thoroughfare Gap near Manassas, Virginia, of "typhoid fever." Another brother, Private William H. Nunn enlisted with his two brothers on June 13, 1861, and was present until October 1864.

The Nunns were part of the "Mountain Boys" that enlisted on May 29, 1861, in Danbury, Stokes County, North Carolina. The men traveled to nearby Danville, Virginia, where they became Company F of the 21st North Carolina Infantry Regiment (11th North Carolina Volunteers). The regiment included men from Davidson, Surry, Forsyth, Stokes, Rockingham, and Guilford counties.

Andrew Nunn enlisted as a Private at age 26. Other than reported sick in October 1861, his early time in the war was not memorable. Eleven months later, his compatriots elected him 3rd Lieutenant on April 26, 1862. By June 1, he was in the hospital at

Mount Jackson. He returned to duty and received promotion to 2nd Lieutenant on August 28.

The area around Winchester was not lucky for Andrew Nunn. Two years later as part of the 2nd Corps of the Army of Northern Virginia under General Jubal Early in Lewis's Brigade on July 20, 1864, he received a wound in the left thigh that broke his femur. Family tradition holds that he lost his leg. His luck ran out at Stephenson's Depot, when Union forces captured him. He spent the rest of the war in either Federal Hospitals or Prisoner of War Camps.

On May 9, 1865, Nunn was at Fort McHenry, Maryland, where Frances Scott Key received his inspiration to write the Star Spangled Banner five decades earlier. Union General Lewis Wallace, who later wrote *Ben Hur,* signed the order transferring Nunn from the General Hospital in Baltimore. On June 24, Nunn took the Oath of Allegiance and was released ending Andy Nunn's Civil War.

Few references to the Civil War were mentioned on The Andy Griffith Show except for one memorable episode "The Loaded Goat" from 1963. Sheriff Andy Taylor tells a lady, who called the Sherriff's office, that the blasting she is hearing out on the highway is not the Yankees attacking Mayberry and he assures her that the South is still holding on to Richmond, Virginia, the Capital of the Confederates States of America.

Years later, the daughter of his younger brother Samuel named her only son after the two Nunn brothers. Geneva Nunn called him Andy Samuel Griffith. He went on to be the most famous person to come from Mount Airy, Surry County, North Carolina.

Civil War General J. E. B. Stuart was born just outside Mount Airy in Patrick County, Virginia, where Andy Griffith's mother grew up. This author led the effort to save part of Stuart's Birthplace, the Laurel Hill Farm, in the early 1990s.

Mayberry Trading Post along the Blue Ridge Parkway
in Patrick County near Meadows of Dan and Mabry Mill.

Mayberry Presbyterian Church, one of the rock churches made famous by Reverend Robert Childress, below, and the book *The Man Who Moved A Mountain.*

Several years ago, I found myself rummaging through the papers of the Patrick County Courthouse. As a lark, I looked up the last name Griffith and, lo and behold, there was a marriage license dated August 22, 1925, between Carl Griffith (1894-1975), a laborer, age 30, the son of John D. and Sallie Griffith of Mount Airy and Geneva Nannie Nunn (1899-1986), age 26, the daughter of Sam and Mary Jophina Cassell Nunn of Patrick County. The Reverend J. S. Rodgers of the Methodist South Church married the couple in Patrick County, probably in the town formerly known as Taylorsville, now Stuart, Virginia, on August 22, 1925. John Clark of the Circuit Court of Patrick County filed the document.

Mary Jophina (Jopina or Jossina or "Jo Pinney") Cassell Nunn (1866-1938) was the daughter of Peter Cassell and Nancy J. Rogers. Samuel "Babe" Nunn (ca. 1850-1905) was the son of John and Scenna Phillips Nunn. Andy Griffith's grandparents were married on February 14, 1886, in Stokes County, North Carolina, and are buried at Old Hollow Primitive Baptist Church Cemetery in Mount Airy.

In 1925, Samuel Walter Nunn owned 122 acres, nine miles from the courthouse in Stuart. The family cemetery is located near Virginia Route 631 between Kibler Valley, where the Dan River rolls off the Blue Ridge and Fall Creek.

Sam Nunn ran a sawmill on Fall Creek, a tributary of the Dan River near where the Mount Airy and Eastern Railroad, "The Dinky" ran from Mount Airy to Kibler Valley in Patrick County, Virginia. One story told to me by the late Colonel James Love of Patrick County was that Andy's grandfather murdered a man and made a deathbed confession about it.

Fall Creek falls from the Blue Ridge Mountains before making its way to the Dan River near the Command Sergeant Major Zeb Stuart Scales Bridge on Highway 104, the Ararat Highway. This author worked to get the bridge named for his neighbor, Scales, who was the most decorated non-commissioned officer to serve in the United States military from Patrick County. Up on the mountain plateau is a small community named

Mayberry. The center of the area is the Mayberry Trading Post, the location of a store since 1858.

Mayberry was once the site of a general store, tannery, brickyard, barbershop, gristmill, and a post office first run by Confederate Veteran Jehu Barnard of the 50th Virginia Infantry and others from 1872 until 1922. One family story tells that Mayberry comes from a Colonel Charles Mayberry, a militia captain, who came into the area in 1809, but there were multiple Mayberrys both named George in 1791 when Virginia cut Patrick County out of its eastern neighbor Henry giving Virginia's first governor Patrick Henry the ability to see his name on a map.

Today, the Blue Ridge Parkway crossing Mayberry Creek rolls by the Mayberry Trading Post just a few miles from Meadows of Dan, Virginia, and the famous Mabry Mill. Mayberry is also the home to one of the rock churches made famous by the Reverend Robert "Bob" Childress in the book *The Man Who Moved a Mountain*. It is the only Childress church in Patrick County and the first one he converted from wood to rock.

Patrick County has a claim to the "Real Mayberry." Jerry Bledsoe's book *Blue Horizons: Faces and Places from a Bicycle Journey Along the Blue Ridge Parkway* published in 1993 tells a story from the time the parkway construction began. Addie Wood of the Mayberry Trading Post said Sam Nunn brought ginseng to sell and brought his grandson, a boy named Andy Griffith. Carl Griffith, Andy's father, was a visitor as well. Addie was sure that this Mayberry was the Mayberry on the television show. "I'm confident that he did. His mother was raised within seven miles of here, and Andy's father I know beyond doubt came to the store here and brought him when he was just a little boy. Andy's mother told me that."

So was Mayberry the inspiration many years later for the name of the town on *The Andy Griffith Show*? Maybe it was a good memory a boy had of his maternal grandfather. As Andy might say, "It sure sounds like it, doesn't it?" In his papers at the University of North Carolina at Chapel Hill Andy Griffith has a copy of the section of Jerry Bledsoe's book with a giant circle around the part about Mayberry Trading Post.

Cape Fear and Yadkin Valley Railroad.

Train with load of Mount Airy Granite.

Mount Airy Depot, then and now in 2012.

The train came to Mount Airy on June 20, 1888, and everything changed. Before that day, the sleepy town at the foot of the Blue Ridge Mountains was a place for growing tobacco and agricultural products. There was a giant outcropping of granite that many thought was useless, but the train changed that too as now there would be a way to transport it out of the place that today is the "Granite City."

Before the train came, the Siamese Twins, Eng and Chang Bunker walked the streets of Mount Airy before it was even a city, which occurred in 1885. Future Civil War General James Ewell Brown "Jeb" Stuart, who was born and grew up just across the line in Patrick County, Virginia, walked the streets of Mount Airy. The Stuarts like people today in southwest Virginia came to town for church, to pick up the mail, or just to shop.

Several businessmen from the region in Virginia and North Carolina including William and Jesse Moore, Winston and Joseph Fulton, Julius Gray, D. W. C. Benbow of Greensboro, A. T. Stokes of Richmond, Virginia, K. M. Murchison of New York City,

Washington Williams and E. J. Lilly of Fayetteville, Robert Gray of Raleigh and W. A. Lash of Walnut Cove, North Carolina, wanted to link the beach to the mountains. The Cape Fear and Yadkin Valley Railroad rolled into Mount Airy for the first after leaving Fayetteville at 8 a.m.

On that Wednesday morning, over 5,000 people were in town and a parade began on North Main Street and ended at the site of the Rockford Street School, where today the Andy Griffith Playhouse is all that is left of the structure. The Governor of North Carolina, Alfred Moore Scales, a Democrat from Reidsville was the guest speaker.

The train changed everything, giving a transportation route for the granite coming out of the town. Soon furniture and textiles dominated the scene in Mount Airy and the railroad was the highway to send it to the world.

The train station built around 1890 is now abandoned on Granite Street one block from South Street. Within sight of the train station at 181 South Street, Dr. Thomas Worrell delivered Andy Samuel Griffith, who first saw the light of day on June 1,

1926, nearly ten months after his parent's marriage, but he did not get his name for six more days on June 7, 1926. He discovered that while he was born on June 1 his name was not registered until June 7 giving him double birthdays. He was born in his paternal aunt's rented home that no longer exists on South Street in Mount Airy. The baby boy, Andy, slept in a drawer in Grace Moore's rented house shared with her husband, John. Grace and Geneva were sisters. The dotting mother noticed her son had a birthmark on the back of his head. She called it "Andy's Strawberry Patch."

Carl Griffith was a carpenter, who worked in Mount Airy's furniture factories. His son described him as a "wonderful Christian man who had a strong influence on me." Born in 1894, Carl Griffith served in the army from 27-April-1918 until 5-January-1920, which included World War 1. There are stories that he was gassed during the war and suffered from tuberculosis later in life, which included trips to a sanatorium in Winston-Salem.

Carl Lee Griffith was the son of John D. and Sarah Frances Taylor Griffith. (Andy had a grandmother named Taylor with a first name of Sarah.) Sheriff Andy Taylor often talked to the town operator, Sarah, on the phone in Mayberry. Andy's Griffith paternal grandparents are buried in White Plains Baptist Church near the grave of the Siamese Twins, Eng and Chang Bunker.

John descended from William Martin Griffith (1833-1895) and Charity Anne Childress (1834-1902). William's parents were Samuel Griffith and Polly Poor. Charity came from William and Fannie Vest Childress.

Sarah Frances Taylor Griffith was the daughter of Henry Clay Taylor (1843-1900) and Rebecca Ann Simmons (1848-1943). Henry descended from Thomas Judson and Sarah Ellen Boaz Taylor. Rebecca descended from Amos and Nancy Emily Inman Simmons.

In Terry Collin's wonderful book *Andy Griffith: An Illustrated Biography*, he writes that the Griffith Family left Mount Airy to live with Geneva's mother in Ohio. Gone for "roughly three years," the family moved to High Point, North Carolina, and eventually back to Mount Airy. My grandfather moved his family from Tennessee to High Point and back to Chattanooga before settling in Mount Airy in 1949.

Upon returning to Mount Airy, the Griffiths and the Perrys lived in several places including the Highland Park section on Huston Street with Geneva's sister, and again on Rockford Street before buying a house on Haymore Street in 1935. In 1958, Andy Griffith renovated the house. He sold the property in 1966 to the Hale Family and moved his parents to California.

At age five, his mother took him to his first entertainment, a production of Carmen in nearby Winston-Salem. The young boy was taken with the "clapping and clanging and carrying on!" of the production.

Griffith spoke of his parents in 1982. "Each of them gave me at least one special gift besides showing their love for me. My mother's family were all musical; all of them played guitars, banjos, fiddles, and other instruments. My father couldn't carry a tune, couldn't even whistle. But he had the best sense of humor of any man I ever met, and he was a great storyteller…my parents started off with two gifts right off the bat."

Haymore Baptist Church on Rockford Street was home to the Griffiths who lived several blocks away near the water tower shown in the distance in this photo.

The house located at 711 Haymore Street today cost Carl and Geneva Nunn Griffith $435, just several blocks up a steep hill from the Mount Airy Chair Company, where Carl Griffith worked as a mechanic and eventually reaching a foreman's position before he retired at age 65.

Andy Griffith and others often talked about his father such as Griffith's cousin Evin Moore who said, "His daddy was a great joker. There was never any dark moments with Carl Griffith." Andy's first wife, Barbara, said of her father-in-law that he was "one of the funniest men she'd known." The apple did not fall far from the Griffith Family Tree.

"I think my father had an enormous influence on me. He was a Christian man, truly honorable and honest, a fine human being, and he had a magnificent sense of humor...If he could've had a chance, he would've been a really fine actor."

Geneva Nunn Griffith brought her Patrick County musical roots with her and she taught her son to play guitar. Andy Griffith was on the Crooked Road, the Virginia Musical Heritage Trail before anyone thought it up.

One particularly poignant story involves him walking downtown by himself to the florist and buying his mother a small potted plant, which was all he could afford. Geneva cried for three days over the kindness of her only child.

Growing up a working class lad in Mount Airy left scars on Andy Griffith. He did not often talk of those days, but in Our State Magazine in 2003 and other publications, he related some stories about his youth in the "Granite City."

"Growing up in Mount Airy, we were poor people...All during the Depression, almost all the time, my father had a job somewhere. If our factory shut down, he would find one somewhere that was open. He was good at running a band saw, so he'd get the job."

In Parade Magazine in 1990, Andy said, "When I was real young, I didn't much like to work. I didn't like to pull a cross saw and throw wood under the house and things like that. What I did like was listening to The Lone Ranger. When I was working in a factory with my father and I hated, working in the factory, work took up at quarter till eight, and we shutdown at a quarter till five. Now, The Lone Ranger came on at five, Monday, Wednesday and Friday, and we'd just be draggin' along."

"Finally, Dad would say, 'We'd better hurry up. We're gonna miss The Lone Ranger.' So we'd sit together by the radio, and Dad would do something every time. When some character'd say 'Who was that masked man?' 'Then the other person would say, 'That was the L-O-N-E Ranger,' and you'd hear, 'Hiyo, Silver, Away!' My father'd go 'Whooooeee!'"

"Or, if something really astounded him, or if he saw a really pretty woman, he'd do a whole body take, go 'Whooooeee!' and he'd walk out of the room and come back and do it again. Even now, periodically I do a body take or make that sound, just like my dad did."

"I remember that the house had black siding. There were three little rooms, with a bathroom on the back. It was cold in there in the winter. In fact, when it snowed the snow came through the cracks...I remember sleeping on a cot and straw mattress in the kitchen next to the wood stove to stay warm. That was the only room with heat."

"When I got older, I slept in the bedroom under ten quilts. I remember standing in front of the fire place and getting warm before going to bed that was the good life."

Andy said his father left the spigot running one night to keep the pipes from freezing, but the drain backed up and they woke to two inches of ice and had to hammer the ice to use the water. When the city hooked the house up to the sewer, Andy imagined the pipe was a high wire and drove his mother crazy walking it. Carl continued to improve the home including adding a cement underpinning.

School was at the Rockford Street School near the present location of the Andy Griffith Playhouse, the school's auditorium and only building remaining. Andy repeated the third grade twice, not because the teacher liked him so much, but because of the myriad of childhood diseases including the mumps and chicken pox.

"In school I was the patsy that everyone picked on. They would hold me down and call me Andy Gump or Amos and Andy. And I hated, hated, hated it, but at some point, my child's mind recognized that I could control the kind of fun that was being made of me. In this way, it put me in charge of the laughter. So I grew up as a class clown; it was a defense mechanism."

"When I was a kid back in Mount Airy, North Carolina, the other fellas, and worse, the girls used to laugh at me. It seemed to me they laughed at me all the time. Not with me, mind you, but at me. My mama made me wear long underwear, and when we had to change in the gym, the other guys would double over in hysterics. It finally got so I'd dress in the shower or toilet where no one could see me…I was awful shy, scraggly, homely kid,…I wanted to belong like the rest of the kids, but I was embarrassed to express myself or my needs. I don't even think I knew what my needs were. There were times when I thought I wanted to die."

"I guess it took me a long time to find out what I wanted to do. I always looked for a way to function as an individual person.

But I started out a loser. Believe me. I was convinced I was born that way by the time I reached adulthood."

"I wasn't smart, my family wasn't wealthy and I wasn't athletic. In a little town like Mount Airy, if you aren't wealthy or athletic you aren't much. You know what I mean? I had to find something else for myself, something mine."

"The happiest times I spent were in my room by myself, where no one could jeer or poke fun at me. And it happened by chance to make something out of a handicap that so many people let pass by. One day I was a kid with a big hurt…and then I said something funny and made a whole room full of people laugh. They laughed at me and all of a sudden I was in control because I'd made them laugh."

"That was a long time ago, but I've never forgotten the laughter. As long as everyone was going to laugh at me, anyway I might as well put myself in the position where I could control the laughter and turned a disadvantage into an advantage, and in doing it, I changed my whole life."

The event that changed Andy Griffith occurred on the stage of what is today the Andy Griffith Playhouse, when he was in the third grade. The person responsible was Albert McKnight, who sat next to Andy in homeroom. The teacher assigned Albert a poem to read representing their class in the assembly. Andy sat on the aisle and when the principal called for the next presentation, he stood up. Albert did not move. Andy found himself standing alone in the big room.

In Andy's own words, here is what happened. "I don't know to this day what made me do it. I guess I was just plumb tired of being made a fool of. But I marched up to the stage and started reciting the poem we'd learned. In between the line, I'd make little comments of my own on what I thought of the poem and the person who wrote it, and they started laughing. I found out I could get them to laugh or listen whenever I wanted them to. What an experience, that great sea of laughter. From that time on, no one kidded me because they knew I could whip them verbally. And, most important, I knew it…A lot of us, most of us, I guess, had unhappy experiences as kids, and the secret is not to just overcome them, but to make the most of them. After all, experience is a dead loss if you can't sell it for more than it cost you."

There is another version Andy and another student were to sing "Put On Your Old Gray Bonnet," but the other student did not show. Griffith only knew the chorus, but that did not stop him. He sang the chorus slow and then fast causing the auditorium to erupt with laughter. Griffith realized he was in control of the situation and a star was born.

Put on your old grey bonnet

With the blue ribbon on it,

While I hitch old Dobbin to the shay,

And through the fields of clover,

We'll drive to Dover,

On our golden wedding day.

Life at the corners of Rockford and Haymore Streets in the shadow of the giant water tower that today has the images of Andy and Opie Taylor going to the "Fishin Hole," was not entirely loneliness. Andy grew up with a group of kids remembered him whether he was building model airplanes or riding his bicycle all over town with his brown and white dog Tippy in a wire basket on the handle bars.

Douglass Benison, Garnett Steele, and Emmett Forrest recalled fond memories of growing up near Andy Griffith and they remained his friends. They fished and played games like "Kick the Can" or told ghost stories at the corner of Rockford and Broad Streets with the other kids in the neighborhood.

Emmett said he could hear Andy coming down the street at night whistling or singing from his voice or music lessons. One imagines that image transferred to the television show years later of the simple joy of a boy growing up walking down the street or to the fishing hole with his son whistling.

Among his friends was James Kingsbury, who once rescued Andy by telling Geneva that some boys tied Andy up in the Old Tabernacle Church. He said that Andy's mother was "serious with no sense of humor with kids." She was pretty and well dressed. Carl Griffith loved to garden, made woodcrafts, and refinished furniture. James was the son of Anderson and Beatrice Kingsbury. Yes his mother was named Bea, like Aunt Bea.

Kingsbury told of the days growing up in Mount Airy with Andy Griffith. It was a time when you played Rag Bag Ball, made kites out of sticks, newspapers, flour, water, and tails from sheets, swam in Lovill and Stewart's Creek, and roamed the streets in shooting out streetlights with slingshots. A slingshot can get a boy in trouble as Opie Taylor found out when he killed the mother bird in a favorite episode of *The Andy Griffith Show*.

Kingsbury told of riding bikes down the steps of the Methodist Church on Rockford Street. There was a "Big Gulley" on Creed Street that the boys rode limber trees down to the ground and built a fire to roast corn and apples. They played football in the churchyard and stole watermelons.

Another friend from Andy's youth was Thomas Garnett Steele. He told of building models of the USS *North Carolina* battleship with Griffith. This author remembers trips to Mount Airy to buy a model of the same ship downstairs at Roses on Main Street on weekly Saturday trips to town.

Andy saved his money to buy an Ocarina, a "Sweet Potato" pipe. Wikipedia says, "The ocarina is an ancient flute-like wind instrument. Variations do exist, but a typical ocarina is an enclosed space with four to twelve finger holes and a mouthpiece that projects from the body. It is often ceramic, but other materials may also be used, such as plastic, wood, glass, clay, and metal."

Steele showed up on the show *This Is Your Life* on March 25, 1971, when Griffith was the subject, much to Griffith's chagrin at first. Steele told of he and Andy letting the air out of some guy's tires, but at the fourth tire they realized the guy was in the car and they spent the rest of the evening pumping up the tires.

The boys took blocks of wood from the furniture factory and made them into cars, trucks, and other toys including model airplanes. "Under Andy's house it was very dry and we would build roads play there when it rained. Our cars and trucks were made of wood his father used for kindling."

They played "King of the Mountain" in a big gully on Creed Street. There were persimmon wars similar to snowball fights and playing "Fox and Dog," a group hide and seek.

Andy Griffith grew up a Baptist at Haymore Baptist Church, the same church this author grew up attending, just a few blocks from his home on Haymore Street north on Rockford Street, where he joined the young people's group to do his "early courting." Soon his interest in learning to play an instrument took him to another church on the other side of town and his life changed again.

While at Haymore Baptist Church, Andy Griffith accepted Jesus Christ as his Lord and Savior. He later recounted, "God has been part of my decision and the cause of my success." His Sunday School teachers were Ruth Gentry, Luther McMillian, Ruby Wagoner, Wheeler Gough, and Katherine Moody. His contemporaries Emmett Forrest and Bill Chandler attended Haymore too. Griffith was famous for singing *"Jesus Loves Me"* so loud and out of tune that people would turn and stare. He sang solos on hymns like *"Sweet Hour of Prayer"* and served as the bell ringer. At age 11, he played a farmer in a Christmas play, which was probably his first time acting in public.

This author remembers well ringing that same bell to call people to the morning service at 11 o'clock and acting in the Christmas play when being over the moon one of the McMillian twins.

Steele spoke of Andy's favorite food, the hot dog. Apparently, the Blue Bird Café had the best hot dogs in town. Pete Owens, the owner sold beer and would not let the kids eat where beer was sold, so they had to go outside to eat. The Snappy Lunch was usually crowded and the owners were "strict on kids."

The back problems that would cause Griffith problems later in life occurred about this time. Floyd Pike, who became famous for his electrical company was dating Emmett Forrest's sister and put up a knotted rope for the boys to swing. Griffith fell from it and hurt his back. Steele said, "I think that could be one of the reasons he was deferred from service" in the U. S. Military.

The kids played football across the street from Haymore Baptist Church and baseball on Reddic Field, where the City Hall is today. Today, where the large water tank painted with Andy and

Opie Taylor on the side was the site of kite flying by Andy and his

friends. Such was life growing up on Haymore Street.

**Grace Moravian Church on North Main Street, where Andy
Griffith met Reverend Mickey to get trombone lessons.**

"Woosh! Screech!" He heard him before he saw him. Reverend Edward T. Mickey, Jr. recalled years later in an article for *The Wachovia Moravian.* The bicycle came to a fast and loud stop at the back door of the Grace Moravian Church at the corner of North Main and Old Springs Road in Mount Airy, North Carolina.

It was a Wednesday in February 1942. Mickey had just finished teaching a group of a dozen children from his congregation the "horn." He wanted a "church band to play chorales for special services," but things were not going very well that day as the children were not much interested and the preacher expressed feeling a little down about the prospects.

That day the whole world was feeling a little down as World War II was in full fruition. In the Philippines, forces of the United States were fighting the Battle of Bataan against the Japanese. The British lost Singapore considered the worst loss in the history of the empire that once ruled the seas. The forces of the Soviet Union, our allies, pushed the German Nazi forces back from

Kursk signaling the beginning to the end of their offensive in Russia. President Franklin D. Roosevelt signed Executive Order 9066 creating "Exclusionary Zones" on both coasts that would lead to the United States government placing citizens of Japanese descent into internment camps questioning their loyalty to the U. S.

Grace Moravian Church started in 1923 when Brother Charles D. Crouch began preaching. In April 1925, 96 people received baptism and the corner stone of the building was laid on September 13, 1925. In May 1929, Brother John Sprinkle took over preaching until 1933 when Reverend Mickey arrived.

In the summer of 1941, before war came to Pearl Harbor, *Birth of the Blues* starring Bing Crosby and Mary Martin was released to moviegoers. Andy Griffith sat watching it in one of Mount Airy's downtown theaters when he saw the trombone player. He was hooked and began to save his money working for $6 a month sweeping floors in order to buy a $33 instrument a silver plated tenor trombone from the Spiegel Catalog.

"My daddy couldn't afford it. He fed me and clothed me, but he couldn't stretch his pay far enough to buy me a musical instrument…I got the trombone and I was the happiest boy in all North Carolina."

This author remembers spending one incredibly hot summer in a tobacco field to save enough money to buy a guitar. Did Andy and this author have the same goal in mind, girls? I think so.

"You the preacher here?" said the "rawboned boy of sixteen with curly, blond hair" sitting "astride" the bicycle. Mickey answered affirmatively. "You teach horn?" Again, Mickey answered positively "inwardly groaning" thinking "O Lord, here's another one!"

Mickey took the initiative stating, "I teach the young folks here at the church." The boy replied, "You teach me? I'll pay you." Mickey replied he could not take pay for doing his job in the church and asked the young man, "Why do you want to learn to play a horn?" The boy replied, "So I can lead a swing band."

The conversation continued with Mickey knowing he was digging his hole deeper. "What kind of horn do you want to learn to play?" The boy replied, "Trombone." Mickey saw a way out of his conundrum. "I don't know anything about trombone. All I could do would be to go through an instruction book with you."

"I got an instruction book." the boy replied. As if in a war of wits with his young antagonist, Mickey said, "You'll have to have a horn" hoping that since he did not see one he could get out of this easily, but the boy responded, "I got a horn." "Where did you get it?" asked the preacher. "Spiegel's" responded the boy. Mickey gave up and said to the boy, "Well, come again next Wednesday and bring your horn. We'll see what we can do." Mickey thought to himself that the boy would not ride the bike two miles across town "for long to do this," but Edward T. Mickey, Jr. like many other people in Mount Airy soon learned of the determination of Andy Griffith.

The following Wednesday in February 1942, there was young Andy on a bicycle with a trombone. Mickey wrote, "…all three combined with enthusiasm for life in quantity enough for half a dozen boys," but he was still not convinced of Griffith's conviction. He did not want to buy instruction books until he knew for sure the young man was in it for the long haul.

Mickey sent Griffith home with a musical scale written on a piece of paper so the preacher could study the trombone book. The next week Griffith came back with the scale "note perfect" as Mickey recalled. He gave Griffith the instruction book with a lesson and he returned the next week with his lesson "note perfect. After three weeks, Griffith asked, "Is that all? I can do more." Mickey gave him two lessons, which he brought back the next week "note perfect."

Reverend Mickey inquired of his young music student when he had time to practice as Griffith's progress obviously took many hours to hone his skill. Andy Griffith responded, "Well, I tell you: I've got my school work; and I've got my studying; and I've got my paper route; and I've got my church work. And that doesn't leave me much time, so I've been getting up about five o'clock in the morning to practice!" Mickey wrote, "My heart went out to the neighbors until I realized that the neighbors also got up about 5 a.m. to go to work."

Andy soon joined the band for rehearsals on Monday nights. During intermission, he took the time to learn the other instruments. Mickey wrote that he and the other members of the band got a bonus "his zest for life and for what he was doing caught on with the rest. The whole group, and yes, the director also, came out of the doldrums, which had enveloped it."

For the next few years, the World would fight a war, while Reverend Mickey and his new student carried on with their own studies of music and singing. Young Griffith did not like to sing in the choir at first saying it was "too sissy," but soon he could not "sing enough." Mickey became concerned about Andy spending so much time away from his church, Haymore Baptist on Rockford Street, but soon the whole Griffith Family joined Grace Moravian.

After joining Grace Moravian Church, Griffith tells about the Easter Sunrise Service that started at three in the morning. "We'd ride around on the back of a truck with our trumpets and trombones waking everybody up and then we'd all go to the church yard and just wait. And then, just as the sun started to crack, the preacher would come out of the church. He'd be all dressed in white and everything would be very quiet. 'The Lord is risen,' he'd say. 'The Lord has risen indeed.' And then we'd march to the graveyard and sing hymns. Some were quiet and some were jubilant, but they were all beautiful."

In 1944, Reverend Mickey left Mount Airy for a congregation in Raleigh, North Carolina. That same year when Griffith left for college, thirty guests including the Youth Fellowship of Grace Moravian church met on a Tuesday evening to say goodbye to Andy. He was accepted as a candidate for the ministry by the Provincial Elders Conference of the Moravian Church South, which included four years at Chapel Hill and three years at the Moravian Theological Seminary in Bethlehem, Pennsylvania. "Andy sang several selections and played a trombone solo."

The preacher followed the career of his student and returned to Mount Airy in 1957 when Griffith's first movie *A Face in the Crowd* premiered on "Andy Griffith Day" invited by the Chamber of Commerce. Reverend Mickey stayed in contact with Andy Griffith visiting him in Manteo, North Carolina, or meeting him on his infrequent trips to Raleigh.

Years later, local educator and historian, Ruth Minick, wrote of another story, possibly apocryphal of the appreciation Andy Griffith had for the man who got him started in "show business." In a telephone conversation, Mickey bemoaned the fact he did not have a fourteen-year-old boy to mow his grass. Time passed and one day an "unkept figure with cap and dark glasses appeared" at Mickey's door with a riding lawn mower on a truck. The Reverend Mickey told the man that he had not ordered a lawnmower. Mickey called the store and finally got the name of the person who ordered the lawnmower. When he returned to the door with his "bird shot rifle" surprising his deliveryman, Reverend Mickey found his deliveryman was Andy Griffith.

Mickey summed it up this way. "Through the years, Andy's generosity in referring to the Moravian Church and to me as having been a cherished part of his life, has been a source of much enjoyment and appreciation on the part of many of us who have known him. We should not take too much credit for this; it was Andy's doing. Had he not been what he was, and is, in basic character and goodness, he would have been just another of the many in his profession who have lost their ideals and sense of values. He lives under the pressures which the rest of us would find intolerable, and does so without sacrificing his own integrity and Christian character."

Life was not all fun and music for Andy Griffith growing up in Mount Airy. One of the jobs of the church band was cleaning the building. He made up songs, invoking the cloth donated from Spencer's Inc., a maker of children's clothing in Mount Airy known for their light blue buildings that can still be seen downtown. Griffith would sing, "Wash your windows with Dr. Spencer's Underwear."

He worked for his cousin Evin Moore at the Weiner Burger. Moore kept Andy busy mostly washing dishes, but he could make milk shakes and he made, yes, that is right, hot dogs. The hot dog runs through Griffith's life, not the pork chop sandwich.

Andy became interested in girls. Eleanor Powell wrote in the Mount Airy News about Griffith's love life. "The year was 1944. The place was Mount Airy High School. The subject was

Andy Griffith. He was a popular kid on the block with a musical background. He had a teenage girlfriend and all the younger students loved to watch as he turned on the school water fountain for her to get a drink of water. As an eighth-grade freshman, I was fascinated with their courtship."

The object of Andy's desires was a girl named Angie Marshall. "We don't know exactly what Andy Griffith is always saying to Angie Marshall that makes her have that far away look in her eye, but we can imagine that it is something like this, 'Whither thou goest, I will go.'"

Near the end of his career at Mount Airy High School, Robert Merritt, who went on to run Renfro Corporation in Mount Airy, recalled how "shocked" they were that Andy agreed to sing at the Senior Banquet. "In high school, Andy never attracted much attention as far as I can remember. Nothing in his manner suggested a career in acting, but about halfway thought the program Andy sang "Long Ago and Far Away." During a moment of stunned silence, someone expressed our surprise by exclaiming 'Gollee ol' Ange can sing' Long and enthusiastic applause followed. He consented to an encore and another one...Years later, I was not surprised by his success on stage."

The monthly newsletter of the MAHS Journalism class stated, "At the Senior Banquet, many girls were swooning to Andy's singing of Long Ago. To top this, some of the boys were too!" Another girl wrote, "The girls simply swoon when Andy Griffith sings I can't decide whether he is like Frank Sinatra or Nelson Eddy."

Andy graduated Mount Airy High School on May 30, 1944, in the same auditorium that bears his name today. He is described as a member of the Glee Club and Athletic Club, having played basketball. He liked music most and dislikes work. "His second ambition is to have a wife and six children. He plans to enter the Navy next year."

In 2005, Griffith said, "When I was in high school, I was not athletic, we didn't have money, and I was not a good student. But when music came into my life, with the trombone and the singing I became somebody."

"Dale Yeatts welcomed Betty Lynn, who played Thelma Lou on *The Andy Griffith Show* , to the Mayberry Trading Post in 2009. Ms. Lynn graciously signed the photo of their meeting. Along the Blue Ridge Parkway in Patrick County, Virginia, on the banks of Mayberry Creek and within sight of the Mayberry Presbyterian Church.

Andy Griffith left Mount Airy in 1944 to attend the University of North Carolina at Chapel Hill. His plan was to become a Moravian preacher and he felt great pride about his accomplishments, as he was the first in his family to attend college. Again, this parallels to my own father, who grew up poor, the oldest son of working class people who came to Mount Airy to work in the textile mills and who was the first in his family to attend college.

Arriving in Chapel Hill, Griffith encountered Edwin S. Lanier, the self-help officer for the university, who got Andy a job as a busboy in the cafeteria for $8, of which $5 was for tuition and $3 to live on with free breakfast. Carl Griffith's boss Raymond Smith, Jr. claimed he helped pay for Andy's education as well. Remembering his financial dire straits at Carolina, Griffith in 1972 started a scholarship of $25,000 for sophomores, juniors or seniors majoring in drama or music.

He wrote in his first letter home to his parents that there were boys singing under a tree outside his dorm room, but "I didn't have the courage to go join them."

One funny story from his time living in Room 33 in the Steele Dorm was that Griffith slept so soundly that an alarm clock would not wake him up. He hung a rope tied to his ankle out the window and friends would tug on it as they passed early in the morning to wake him until he came to the window to let them know he was stirring. A problem occurred one Saturday night when a group walked by after attending a party and nearly jerked Griffith out the window.

He started as sociology major, but after failing a few classes and becoming bored with the classes in his major, he realized that he needed to go in another direction. He did break one record at Chapel Hill. "My counselor, a lady, called me in and said, 'Andy, very few people fail political science once, but nobody fails it twice.' I guess that was the only record I ever broke at Chapel Hill."

Andy went to the Bishop of the Southern Province of the Moravian Church to get permission to specialize in music. He returned to Chapel Hill, changed his major to music, and started playing slide trombone in the band. He later switched to E-flat bass sousaphone. He sang in the glee club and started thinking about acting in the Carolina Playmakers of the Drama Department.

During this time, a back injury from his youth began to bother him resulting in a trip to Duke Medical Center, where they discovered his back was out of alignment. The diagnosis placed him in a brace that cost $30. Griffith found there was a state program for indigent students with physical disabilities for which he qualified.

With his medical and financial problems solved, he focused on his music and his acting starting to perform Gilbert and Sullivan securing the role of Don Alhambra del Bolero in *The Gondoliers*. He would perform in every musical produced while he was a student in Chapel Hill including the lead role of Sir Joseph Porter in *HMS Pinafore*.

Paul Young of the choral department gave Griffith free voice lessons for working as the music librarian, which involved taking care of the music books of the Glee Club. This relationship lasted for five years.

Often hitchhiking, Griffith returned to Mount Airy to perform in the auditorium that today bears his name as part of the Mount Airy Operetta Club performing such roles such as a judge in *Trial by Jury* and Kezal in *The Bartered Bride*.

The biggest opportunity for Griffith during this time was with *The Lost Colony* in Manteo, North Carolina, on Roanoke Island. For the next seven summers, Griffith and his fellow actors lived in a deserted Navy air base built during World War II. He started in supporting roles, but for the last five years, he was Sir Walter Raleigh. He was so taken with the area along the Outer Banks that he made it his permanent home.

Another opportunity presented itself to Griffith and that was to perform standup routines in comedy clubs along the seashore. He began with "The Preacher and the Bear" and started doing Shakespeare parodies including "Hamlet."

During this time, he met Barbara Bray Edwards in the Carolina Players at Chapel Hill. The daughter of J. S. Edwards of Troy, North Carolina, Barbara was a graduate of Converse College in South Carolina with a music degree. Andy graduated with a bachelor of music degree from UNC-Chapel Hill in 1949. Among his endeavors was president of the chapter of Phi Mu Alpha Sinfonia, America's oldest fraternity for men in music.

It was love at first song. Griffith became so smitten after hearing Barbara sing that he proposed three days after meeting her. The two went to Manteo to act in *The Lost Colony*, where Barbara played Elizabeth Dare. They were married on August 22, 1949, in the Little Log Chapel. Griffith said that he "married in a copy of an Anglican chapel by a Methodist minister to a Baptist maiden while a Roman Catholic vibraphonist played the pump organ."

After the summer job was over and graduation from UNC-Chapel Hill, Andy Griffith needed a job. Thanks to Clint Britton, the stage manager of *The Lost Colony*, he found one teaching drama and music at Goldsboro High School. The young couple moved to 1208 East Mulberry Street in Goldsboro to begin their married life. Barbara served as musical director for two churches in the town.

After his first year, Griffith began to recruit students from the freshman for his class. He soon realized he was not the greatest teacher. "I knew my subject, but I couldn't seem to pass on my knowledge. There were some gifted kids in my classes, and I felt they were entitled to the best possible instruction. Well, I didn't feel I was the best possible instructor…I couldn't handle the kids. I wasn't a good teacher."

"I was happy as a child. I was happy as a teenager. I was happy as a young adult. I never had capital, but I was never unhappy because of that. When I discovered I could entertain I worked hard at it. It's the only thing I do well. I can't be a company director. I can't be an accountant. I can't make furniture, but I can entertain."

Next came a futile attempt with the Paper Mill Playhouse in Milburn, New Jersey. Katherine Warren of Goldsboro was teaching the young Griffiths singing. A friend of Warren offered the Griffiths a ride to New Jersey. The couple stayed a week in the

Statler Hotel, watched the other performers, and "got scared to death by the city." Barbara sang "In the Still of the Night" and he sang "Dancing in the Dark."

"Someone standing around there told me my voice was overly brilliant, almost unpleasantly so. I didn't mind so much. In my own heart, I believed it. So I decided to quit singing and start telling jokes."

He got a job doing his standup act between acts at the Raleigh Little Theater thanks to its director Ainslie Pryor. Griffith later said, "I always had a mental block about school. I was always afraid I wouldn't measure up…I'm still trying to do is measure up. I'm still trying to prove something to that man who said I couldn't sing. I believed him. I knew now I would never be a singer. There is a moment when the truth comes to you, and you wonder what you are going to do next."

"The Deacon Andy Griffith" continued with "The Preacher and the Bear," a hymn "In the Pines" and others. Barbara convinced him to play the "Rotary Club Circuit" with her and they began an act together singing, dancing, guitar playing and monologues with piano Larry Stith joining them for $15. They charged $75 plus mileage for their "Unique Entertainment."

They took money from their teacher retirement fund and obtained loans from Mount Airy friends Jim Yokley and Robert Smith to start their venture. They moved back to Chapel Hill, and worked up a promotional brochure including photos. Griffith describes it as a "time of discovery."

Their first job was at the Asheboro Rotary Club in October 1952. Program Chairman W. A. "Red" Underwood invited them because he knew Barbara to their annual reception and dinner for new teachers in Asheboro Schools. Underwood later said it was the "best 50 bucks that the Rotary ever spent on a program."

Barbara described those times. "We had hard times. We've gone hungry, but we were never destitute. Something always happened to help us. We didn't worry when we gave up the security of teaching and that weekly paycheck. We just knew we could make out all right. When we didn't have money, we always felt rich. Our aspirations were bigger than making money and we had faith. We had faith in each other!"

During this time, Griffith developed his famous monologue "What It Was, Was Football" about the "Deacon" encountering his first college football game. Today, it plays before every home football game at Chapel Hill. He claimed he came up with it driving between gigs based on a dirty joke that Vic Huggins, a Chapel Hill hardware store owner told him. No doubt sitting in the band during college where he played tuba and observing the crowd and the game were also the inspiration for the comedy routine.

He performed the monologue at the Jefferson Standard Life Insurance Company convention in September 1953 in Greensboro, North Carolina. Orville Campbell recorded it for $20 and released it on his Colonial Records with Romeo and Juliet on the B-side splitting the profits with Griffith. The record came out on November 14, 1953, the day the Tarheels lost to Notre Dame 34 to 14.

Hal Cooke, a Sales Manager for Capitol Records, became interested in the recording and sent out Richard O. Linke from New York City. Linke eventually became Griffith's personal manager.

Lee Kinard the long time icon of WFMY in Greensboro told a story on air after Griffith's death. Apparently, Kinard could never get Andy to come on the *Good Morning Show* for an interview, but he did encounter him at WABZ in Albemarle, North Carolina, as a 21 year old, on a PR tour. The program director was named Gomer Ledge. It appears Andy Griffith never forgot anything or anyone he encountered.

The success of "Football" allowed the Griffiths to pay off their debts. They moved to New York City into an apartment in Kew Gardens in Queens at the end of 1953. Linke signed Griffith to a contract with the William Morris Agency, which resulted in an unfortunate performance on *The Ed Sullivan Show* that was a failure.

Griffith needed some seasoning that he accomplished on the Southern night club circuit with shows all over the South from Florida to Texas and beyond including performances with the future "King of Rock and Roll," Elvis Presley. He saw Burl Ives, the man many of us know as the snowman on *Rudolph The Red Nosed Reindeer,* but Griffith described his standup routine as a "master at work." Ives said that the eyes reflect what you feel and that Andy Griffith reflected fear.

During his travels, Griffith received a copy of Mac Hyman's novel *No Time For Sergeants*. In 1955, the U. S. Marine Corps television broadcast of *No Time For Sergeants* appeared on the U. S. Steel Hour on ABC with Griffith in the role of Will Stockdale. Many believe *Gomer Pyle U. S. M. C.* came from NTFS.

A Broadway version followed when Producer Maurice Evans saw Griffith's performance. Andy became the only one to move from the television version to the Broadway version, which premiered on October 20, 1955.

Griffith said of playing Will Stockdale "Will was the most Christian human imaginable. All of the comedy came from that. It wasn't so much that the character was corn pone, it was that he was so honest and dedicated to doing right that it clashed constantly with the new society he was thrust into…"

While comedy was carrying Griffith's career, he knew he could do more and that chance came when Elia Kazan offered him the role of a lifetime as Lonesome Rhodes in *A Face in the Crowd*. Andy Griffith left the Broadway stage for the big screen and what many believe to be the best performance of his career.

Years earlier, Bob Armstrong wrote a three-act play that Griffith played the lead. Armstrong was in the stage play *Cat On A Hot Tin Roof* in New York City directed by Elia Kazan. Armstrong recommended Griffith.

Of making the movie Griffith said, "It was three months out of my life I wouldn't swap for anything…He taught me how to relate everything I had ever heard or read to what I was doing at the moment." Before this, Griffith felt he was not cut out for dramatic roles, but his family did not think so. His cousin Evin Moore said, "They talk about Andy and his acting. He aint acting! He's just being Andy Griffith like he always was. Now, if he ever starts acting', you'd see something!"

On his birthday in 1957, Mount Airy welcomed home a favorite son for "Andy Griffith Day" with a parade and several events. The cover of this book shows the happy Griffith family on that day. This event is often cited as the day that turned Andy against his hometown, but the written record does not back that conclusion.

The Mount Airy News reported that on June 1, 1957, 15,000 people came out to see Andy Griffith. He flew into Winston-Salem's Smith Reynolds Airport about 9:20 a.m. A 25-vehicle motorcade left the airport at 11 a.m. arriving at 1 p.m. for lunch at Reeves. *A Face in the Crowd* played at the Earle Theater at 3:30 p.m. and 8:30 p.m. Griffith received a Proctor Silex electric toaster from Surry Representative, Joe Fowler, Jr., Mount Airy was once "the toaster capital of the world."

Griffith wrote Mayor W. Frank Carter, Jr. afterwards. "I'm ashamed I've waited so long to thank you for the celebration you had for me in Mount Airy. I think the reason is that I just don't know how to thank you. I don't know that I have ever been so overcome by anything. I saw people that I haven't seen in years, and it's a real joy to know that Barbara and I have their concern and good wishes...For a while I wondered why you did all that, but I realized you did it because you are proud and that makes us proud. We will try to live a life that will continue to make you feel that way."

Eleanor Powell of the Mount Airy News wrote after Griffith's death. "Some of his classmates from prominent families thought they were a bit better than he and completely ignored the Surry County native until the actor made it to the Big Apple and Hollywood. It was after making his first movie, *A Face in the Crowd*, and starring in *No Time for Sergeants*, some of the local snobs traveled to New York for the grand opening of *No Time For Sergeants*. It was payback time for Andy when the Granite City crowd claimed fame to the actor, requesting a favor to go backstage for autographs. Andy denied their requests. He would not see them nor autograph their programs. I just know he must have had a good feeling after they had treated him with disrespect in earlier days at school."

A visitor to the newspaper website made this comment after the story appeared. "I know at least one delegation from Mt. Airy was received graciously by Andy Griffith backstage in New York at the Broadway theater, my Mom and Dad being part of it. According to them, it was a group of the local dignitaries, including the perennial Mayor Maynard (Beamer), if I recall correctly. They were all nervous about who he would remember, but it was my Mother he singled out first after carefully studying the crowd. 'Why, Miss Graves, how have you been?' he said with a big grin to his former sixth grade English teacher at Mount Airy public schools. She had always remembered him as a talented, personable student whose Father worked with hers in the "Yard"(furniture, lumber). I always thought he used her name as the telephone operator in the series, but could never be sure."

Still another comment from the website. "I saw him once, marching as a Girl Scout in his parade in Mt. Airy for the premiere of the movie *A Face in the Crowd*. He was riding on the back of an open Convertible, grinning widely while passing the marquee on Main Street's movie theater featuring his film. Local bands were marching in his honor as a tribute to his musical interest. Celebrate the success of this Mount Airy Bear!"

So, the real story may never be known as there are people on both sides of the issue. There is no question that many in Mount Airy view Griffith's success with great pride and others who still want to denigrate his accomplishments. He left Mount Airy for New York the day after the celebration, but returned many times.

His proud mother stood across the street sipping Cokes when the matinee was over and signed autographs for people. "She was as proud of him as she could be."

Alma Venable, who now owns the Mayberry Motor Inn that features an Aunt Bee Room, was Geneva's beautician. "I did Andy's mother's hair. She loved to talk about him. Andy was her only son. Andy was just about all she had. And I know that he called her every day until he moved her out to California with him."

During this time, Griffith made the decision not to go home again, but to make his home along the North Carolina coast when he and Barbara purchased 53 acres on Roanoke Island for $30,000.

Near where *The Lost Colony* is still performed, Griffith spoke of his need for "open space" and "No matter what happens, we know that's home, the place we can really be free…wherever else I got to be, but Manteo, that's home."

After more than 300 performances on Broadway, filming began for the film version of *No Time For Sergeants* late in 1957. The following year he filmed *Onionhead*. He appeared on *The Tonight Show* and *The Steve Allen Show* and multiple times a week on the CBS radio network. He went back to Broadway starring in *Destry Rides Again* singing in a role made famous by everyone from silent movie star Tom Mix to Jimmy Stewart and Audie Murphy. Griffith received a Tony Award nomination for his work on the Broadway stage in 1960, his first was in 1956. Strange as it might be to readers. Griffith never received an award for his acting on stage, screen, or television.

In the fall of 1959, Griffith met with his agent Richard Linke and television producer Sheldon Leonard, who was doing *The Danny Thomas Show*. The result of these meetings became

The Andy Griffith Show, which premiered in October 1960 after an initial appearance with Danny Thomas on his show.

Griffith said it best about the character of Sheriff Andy Taylor. "I guess you could say I created Andy Taylor. Andy Taylor's the best part of my mind. The best part of me."

The purpose of this book is not to speak to the television show that brought so much of Mount Airy to Mayberry as many far better books do that. Andy's cousin Evin Moore said it best when describing the show. "Andy never left Mount Airy. He plain took it to Hollywood with him."

While many of the television shows of that time concentrated on the people out in the country like *Green Acres, Petticoat Junction* and the *Beverly Hillbillies, The Andy Griffith Show* was deeper summed by Griffith himself, who said, "We tried to have a little message in every episode."

"What I would like to do, whenever I act or entertain, is to say some small truth…There's no point in doing what you don't enjoy and if you don't do something well, you can't enjoy it."

An article in the 1961 Mount Airy Times, revealed Griffith's life at the time. He spent about 2 ½ months a year in Manteo. His parents stayed with him and his father Carl loved to duck hunt with the 12-gauge shotgun his son bought him. The elder Griffith retired in 1959. Beginning his work life in 1923, he finished as foreman in the machine room. Carl Griffith loved to watch baseball including trips to New York City to watch the World Series and the Yankees.

As for the show that made their son famous, the article states the following regarding his parent's view of it all. "When they first started watching his current show it was difficult for them to grasp just what Andy was about. They understand the story better now."

In April 1966, Andy returned to Mount Airy to move his parents to California to be closer to him. I believe he then encountered my father at the Hospital Pharmacy. He sold his boyhood home for $6,000 to the Hale Family on May 31. Gary York bought the house in 1998 and sold it in May 2001 for $85,000. The Hampton Inn now operates it as a bed and breakfast.

During this visit in 1966, Griffith spoke to school kids at elementary, junior high, and high school including a speech from the Rockford Street School stage that began his career. He signed autographs and got a kiss from Bettsee Smith McPhail.

Carl and Andy Griffith returned to Mount Airy in 1967. "I went back there with my Dad a short while back, and I'm telling you we got lost. There's upwards of towards 10,000 people. You won't believe this, Main Street is one way now."

Griffith tried to leave his popular show in 1967, but CBS lured him back for one last season in 1968. The show morphed into *Mayberry RFD* with Ken Berry in the starring role. It was always this author's opinion that after Don Knotts left the show for a movie career that Andy seemed bored without his long time partner who he worked with stretching back to *No Time For Sergeants*.

Griffith summed up his iconic role saying, "People ask me why it's still as popular. I always said it was because it was based on love."

"They allowed me to write on the show. I had to learn how to handle the script, but they allowed me to write. I did not come up with the ideas, plots, etc., but I often wrote dialogue."

Like many people, Andy Griffith looked back on life with regrets especially about his son's death. He told the television program *Entertainment Tonight*, "I think I'd do everything different." He regretted leaving *The Andy Griffith Show* saying the show was "more my home than my home was."

Scenes from the interior of Haymore Baptist Church, where Andy Griffith first acted in the Christmas play.

Jim Clark of *The Andy Griffith Show* Rerun Watchers Club (TAGSRWC) said it best once. "Mount Airy's not exactly Mayberry, but it's about as close as you can get." No better authority than the man who played Barney Fife, Actor Don Knotts, said in the A&E network show *Biography* that Andy Griffith was heavily involved in the stories and writing the show. With this information, in spite of the many times that Griffith himself has denied it until recently, there is no doubt that he took people and places in his hometown to his television show. This chapter tells about some of them.

In 2003, Griffith talked about how the references he shared were anecdotes he told the writers about growing up in Mount Airy. "I would mention names of people in Mount Airy, and places in Mount Airy like Snappy Lunch, and so the people in Mount Airy got to saying it was based on Mount Airy, and that's gone on so long that I guess it just was based on Mount Airy."

**Corner of Granite and South Streets in Mount Airy
near the site of Andy Griffith's birthplace, now torn down.**

Andy Griffith Playhouse and Andy Griffith Museum.

711 Haymore Street, boyhood home of Andy Griffith was 197 Haymore when he lived there.

The house where Andy Griffith was born was at 181 South Street no longer stands. Located at the intersection of Pine and South Streets, the home was near the train station on Granite Street. Griffith's boyhood home is located at 711 Haymore Street near the intersection with Rockford Street.

The Andy Griffith Playhouse operated by the Surry Arts Council was the site of Griffith's first stage performance as a third grader in what was then the Rockford Street School. He sang, "Put on Your Old Gray Bonnet." In 2002, he performed the song again for his wife, Cindi.

In front of the Andy Griffith Playhouse is the TV Land statue of Andy and Opie Taylor going to Myers Lake to fish from depicted in the opening of *The Andy Griffith Show*. Placed here in 2004, the dedication was one of the few public events Griffith attended in Mount Airy.

Charles Dowell began working at the Snappy Lunch in 1943, bought half the business eight years later and the entire business in 1960, the year *The Andy Griffith Show*, went on the air. The restaurant is known for the "World Famous Pork Chop

Sandwich." Andy Griffith actually ate the hot dogs in the restaurant. Episode #9, "Andy The Matchmaker" mentions the business that started in 1923 when Andy and Barney take the girls to eat.

The Mount Airy News started in 1880 is the only daily newspaper printed today. In Episode #154 "Aunt Bee's Invisible Beau," Sheriff Taylor is reading a real copy of the Mount Airy News.

Charles Dowell and the "World Famous Pork Chop Sandwich." Andy Griffith spoke of the Snappy Lunch in his monologue "Silhouettes," but of having a hot dog.

Grace Moravian Church at the corner of North Main Street and Old Springs Street was the place often sighted where Andy Griffith's career began when he started taking music lessons from Reverend Mickey. Griffith's family later joined the church and a few years before his death he reestablished his connections with the church. It is mentioned in Episode #240 "Barney Hosts a Summit Meeting" as a place to hold the meeting. It is one of the many buildings in Mount Airy made of granite from the North Carolina Granite Quarry.

The athletic teams of Mount Airy High School are the "Granite Bears" for the granite quarry and the many black bears that still roam the area. The school holds numerous state championships in tennis, basketball and football in 2008. Episode #130 "Family Visit," Sheriff Taylor wonders aloud how the Mayberry Bears are doing.

The Mount Airy Furniture Factory is mentioned in Episode #28 "Andy Forecloses" when Lester Scobey attempts to get a job at the Mayberry Furniture Factory. Carl Griffith, Andy's father, worked at the Mount Airy Chair Company, which no longer stands along Factory Street. Andy worked there as a youth and when home from college. The whistles from these operations were heard all over town.

Many mentions of streets in Mount Airy correspond to several episodes in *The Andy Griffith Show*. The intersection of Pine and Main Streets is the center of town. In Episode #99 Ernest

T. Bass Joins the Army," Andy and Barney wait for Bass at this intersection.

Orchard Street/Road is the site of $25,000 stolen from a Raleigh Bank, hidden in a dry well in Episode #228 "Tape Recorder" by Eddie Blake on Ferguson's farm.

Spring Street intersects Rockford Street nearly in front of the Andy Griffith Playhouse. In Episode # 23 "Andy and Opie, Housekeepers," the Stop Sign on Spring Street keeps getting knocked down.

The intersection of Haymore and Rockford Streets, where Andy Griffith, Emmett Forrest, and others sat and told ghost stories was mentioned in the show in Episode #159 "Banjo Playing Deputy."

Banner Street named for the same Banner Family that Bannertown is also named for was mentioned in Episode #5 "Opie's Charity," as a dividing line for fundraising purposes.

In Episode #42 "The Clubmen" Elm Street is the site of another broken Stop Sign for Barney to repair. In Episode #50 "Jail

Break" Andy Taylor's address is 24 Elm Street. In Episode #44 "Sheriff Barney", Fife's address is 411 Elm Street.

In Episode #13 "In Mayberry Goes Hollywood," leaders against the protest of Sheriff Taylor want to cut down the "Signature Oak" to "impress" Hollywood producers. Willow Street in Episode #44 "Sheriff Barney" along with Woods Way are the quietest streets in Mayberry.

The street full of places referenced in *The Andy Griffith Show* is Main Street, where today a thriving tourism economy keeps the downtown area of Mount Airy vibrant. The following are a few the businesses mentioned or with connections.

In Episode #45 "The Farmer Takes A Wife," Sheriff Taylor and Thelma Lou teach farmer Jeff Pruitt etiquette and get him to buy a suit from the men's clothier in Mayberry. In this show, Carl Griffith makes a cameo appearance by walking out of Carroll's of Mayberry. The men's clothier in Mount Airy is F. Rees along Main Street.

The Grand Theater was located on Main Street where Greene Financial is located today. When I was a kid, this was the Western Auto Store. The theater held 739 people and was across the street from the Earle Theater, which still stands today and is operated by the Surry Arts Council. In Episode #50 "Jail Break," shows the Grand in the background of the show.

Another business still on Main Street is Lamm's Drug Store. Ellie Walker (Eleanor Donahue) operated a drugstore in Episode #239 "Opie's Drugstore Job."

Nearby streets contain businesses mentioned on the show. Hutchens Cleaners and Laundry on Spring Street just down the hill from the Andy Griffith Playhouse started in 1939. In Episode #50 "Jailbreak," Sheriff Taylor solves a case "thanks to the remark of the Mayberry Dry Cleaners."

On the opposite side of the Andy Griffith Playhouse, is Moody's Funeral Home along Pine Street that was once Nelson-Moody. In Episode #107 of *Gomer Pyle U. S. M. C.*, a spinoff of *The Andy Griffith Show*, Gomer says the words of the Marine Corps Hymn ("From the Halls of Montezuma to the shores of Tripoli") were on the back of the Nelson Funeral Parlor calendar.

The Nelson-Moody building still stands off Franklin Street on Market Street.

Frances Bavier (Aunt Bee) is remembered at the Mayberry Motor Inn at 501 Andy Griffith Parkway North. Owner Alma and her husband L. P. Venable began collecting items from Bavier's estate in 1990 in Raleigh with a vanity. Several years later, Alma organized her collection into the Aunt Bee Room at the motel. Alma also had a connection to Andy Griffith as she was Andy's mother Geneva's hairdresser and herself dresses up as Aunt Bee. The room has over thirty Bavier items including a twin bedroom suit, eyeglasses, gloves and a dress.

Alma Venable with Goober (Tim Pettigrew), Otis (Kenneth Junkin), and Floyd (Allan Newsome)

Other places in Surry County are mentioned in *The Andy Griffith Show*. Among them is Pilot Mountain known as Mount Pilot in the show. Episode #123 "Fun Girls," are from Mount Pilot and want to take Andy and Barney to the Kit Kat Club. The town is home of the "Miracle Salve," the Trucker's Café, and archrivals of the Mayberry Bowling Team.

Pilot Mountain is a metamorphic quartzite monadnock that rises to 1,400 feet above the piedmont and over 2,400 feet overall within sight of the 3,000 foot Blue Ridge Mountains. The name comes from the Native-American word Jomeokee, for "the Great Guide" or "Pilot."

Another Pilot Mountain connection is seen in Episode #186 "Goober's Replacement." Goober considers leaving Mayberry to work in Mount Pilot to go work for Earlie Gilley's garage. In real life, Earlie's wife Lorraine Beasley Gilley was Griffith's first cousin and he is mentioned in multiple episodes of the show as Andy Griffith Show as "Andy just loved his name."

Dobson is the county seat of Surry County. In Episode #44 "Sheriff Barney," the former tries to find out from a sleeping Otis the location of his still, which leads through Dobson, North Carolina.

Toast, North Carolina along Highway 89 west of Mount Airy is mentioned in Episode #249 "A Girl for Goober," the last show, as a place to test dating services.

Other places mentioned in the environs of Mount Airy include Bannertown, where in Episode #136 "Opie's Fortune" Parnell Rigsby of Bannertown RFD puts an advertisement in the Mayberry Gazette for money he lost in Mayberry. Bannertown is located along Highway 89/Business Highway 52 south and east of town along the Ararat River.

Another place mentioned in the show is Franklin. In Episode #55 "Aunt Bee the Warden," the Gordon Boys have a liquor still in Franklin Hollow. In Episode # 59 "Three's A Crowd," Sheriff Taylor talks about a picnic in Franklin Woods. Nearby places in Virginia are mentioned in the show such as Fancy Gap. Episode #17 "Alcohol and Old Lace" and Episode #155 "Arrest of the Fun Girls" talk of the gap that is "Fancy" because it crosses between two mountains instead of the usual one mountain that a gap traverses.

On the Old Fancy Gap Road is the Blu Vue Motel. Episode #240 "Barney Hosts a Summit Meeting," mentions the banquet room as a possible meeting place for the "East-West Summit." The

Blu Vue was the first motel in Mount Airy where visitors could stay and eat.

Episode #98 "Ernest T. Bass Joins the Army" shows Andy and Barney eating at The Diner. In 1956, The Diner moved to Hillsville, Virginia, up Fancy Gap, where it still operates today just a few doors away from the Carroll County Courthouse, site of the famous 1912 shootout.

The old Mount Airy City Jail.

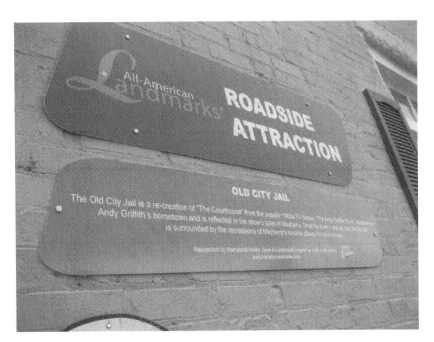

116

117

Melvin Miles, one of the drivers for Squad Car Tours, headquartered at Wally's on South Main Street.

There is Emmett's Fix It Shop and the Mayberry
Courthouse with cannon out front.

120

Outside Mount Airy off Old Highway 601 there is
Turner's Mountain, where in *The Andy Griffith Show*
"Checkpoint Chickie" with "Big 3 5" on the speed limit sign
was on Turner's Grade.

For the Briscoe Darling fans you will remember the horse trough shown here as a flower planter today where he dipped his hat to get some water for the radiator. Mount Airy is the home of the North Carolina Granite Corporation, the largest open-faced granite quarry in the world, shown on the preceding page.

Under the water tower across the street from his boyhood home, Andy Griffith flew kites from a rock now gone.

The steps of the Methodist Church down which Griffith
and friends rode bikes down.

The gulley off Creed Street was the place where Griffith played "King of the Mountain" with his friends.

A very common site on Main Street is the image of Barney Fife played by Don Knotts on the Andy Griffith Show loading his one bullet into his revolver and acting as security for restaurants that bear his name or license plates on many vehicles. Security by Fife!

Every year people by the busload visit Main Street to see the side by side attractions of the Snappy Lunch, "Home of the World Famous Pork Chop Sandwich," and Floyd's City Barber Shop. One of the few real businesses mentioned on the Andy Griffith Show was the Snappy Lunch. The Mayberry Effect that now dominates the town began when the City Barber Shop became Floyd's City Barber Shop.

Mount Airy is a place you can live the good life or shop there after getting a bite just like Sheriff Andy Taylor and Barney Fife at the Blue Bird Diner.

The swing in the yard of the Andy Griffith Homeplace.

Evin Moore, Andy's first cousin and neighbor on Haymore

Street had several connections to the show. Evin's mother Grace

Moore may have been the real Aunt Bee. In Episode #166 "Off to

Hollywood," the Taylors visit Andy's cousin Evin Moore, a Mason

in Asheville, North Carolina. Moore was a Mason in real life. In

Episode #67 "Andy's Rich Girlfriend," Sheriff Taylor talks about

taking Peggy McMillan to the Weiner Burger, which was owned

by Evin Moore. The restaurant was a place where both Andy and

his mother, Geneva Nunn Griffith, worked and was located at the

corner of Rockford and Worth Streets. Geneva worked there when

Carl was sick due to his health troubles from World War I.

Above front row left and right, Elizabeth and Anna Brady at the home their mother Denise Watson Brady lived also the home of Andy Griffith. Below, another view of Andy Griffith Day in 1957 with Carl and Andy Griffith in the back seat.

Only three television shows went out on top among them *I Love Lucy* and *Seinfeld*. When Andy Griffith took off his badge as Andy Taylor for the last time in 1968, he had the most popular show on television. It ran for 249 episodes spinning off shows like *Gomer Pyle USMC* and *Mayberry RFD*.

Andy Griffith struggled to find himself for many years acting in many roles on television, the movies, and even standup routines in Las Vegas and Lake Tahoe, Nevada. He appeared in guest starring roles on everything from *MOD Squad,* to *Sonny & Cher, Hawaii Five-O,* and even *Saturday Night Live*. Several failed attempts at new Andy Griffith Shows occurred.

He starred in television movies such as *Winter Kill* in 1974 as Sheriff Sam McNeill or Sheriff Sam Adams the following year in *Adams of Eagle Lake*. In 1977, he was Police Chief Abel Marsh in *Empty Grave* and *Deadly Game*. The year 1981, brought his memorable performance as Ash Robinson in *Murder in Texas*, for which he received an Emmy nomination. Two years later, he was the bad guy against good guy and Sheriff Johnny Cash in *Murder in Coweta County*.

Eleanor Powell recounted a story about her schoolmate. "I remember sitting at my desk here in the office around the late 1960's when the central telephone rang and over the intercom the receptionist announced, 'Eleanor Greenwood, you have a call coming in from California. It's Andy Griffith.' Waiting with anticipation and all of the reporters listening, Andy, a former high school friend said, 'Eleanor, I need your assistance. My father has passed away and I would like you to place his obituary in The Mount Airy News.' I expressed condolences and we chatted a few minutes before he said good-bye."

It was actually 1975 when Carl Griffith died. That same year, the Surry County Arts Council renamed the Rockford Street School Auditorium the Andy Griffith Playhouse. The following year he received a Star on the Hollywood Walk of Fame. UNC-Chapel Hill recognized Griffith as Distinguished Alumnus in 1977.

Griffith divorced his first wife Barbara in 1972. He married Solica Cassato in 1975 and divorced her in 1981. Griffith returned to his faith during this time stating "…one Christmas when I was living alone. I was very lonely, and I called up somebody…to find out if anybody might be doing The Messiah in Los Angeles…" He found a church in Glendale, California, and asked if he could sing. Griffith started attending and did for years. He attended a Methodist Church in Manteo when back in North Carolina.

Two years later, he married his last wife Cindi Knight. She like Griffith came to Manteo to be in *The Lost Colony* five years before their marriage.

In 1983, Guillain-Barre Syndrome left him paralyzed and recovering through seven months of physical therapy and long-term rehabilitation. He started filming *Matlock* in leg braces due to the illness. The disease started as flu, but turned into "terrible searing pain that ricocheted through my entire body."

"I owe God a lot. Beating that illness and being able to work again. I absolutely love what I do. I was given a gift, and I'm a thankful man, and I try to respect and have it and work on it, help it and know it. That's how I try to pay the Good Lord back."

He turned to friend Leonard Rosengarten, who got him to Northridge Hospital Medical Center in California. He learned to use his mind to control his pain. It took nearly a year for him to recuperate, but he still had permanent pain in both his feet.

Griffith fell on hard times, financially and emotionally. He put his California home up for sale, but got no buyers. He sat in the lobby of the William Morris Agency hoping for a job. He made four television movies including *Return to Mayberry* and the pilot for *Matlock*. The show *Matlock* ran from 1986 until 1995 giving Griffith that rare second hit show. The last three seasons were filmed in Wilmington, North Carolina, allowing him to return to North Carolina permanently.

During this time, he starred as Colonel Ticonderoga in 1985's *Rhustler's Rhapsody* with Tom Berringer. He returned to North Carolina as Victor Worheide in 1984's *Fatal Vision* about Jeffrey McDonald's murder of his wife and children at Fort Bragg.

"Each of us faces pain, no two ways about it. But I firmly believe that in every situation, no matter how difficult, God extends grace greater than the hardship and strength and peace of

136

mind that can lead us to a place higher than where we were before."

In 1992, the Academy of Television Arts inducted Griffith in their Hall of Fame. He received a Grammy Award for Best Southern Gospel, Country Gospel or Bluegrass Gospel Album for *I Love To Tell The Story: 25 Timeless Hymns*. More music followed in 1998 with *Just As I Am: 30 Favorite Old Time Hymns*. His last recording was *The Christmas Guest: Bound for the Promised Land*, a book and CD. The Christian Music Hall of Fame also inducted Andy Griffith.

In 1996, Griffith faced the biggest tragedy of his life when his son, "Sam" passed away. "My son died of an overdose when he was 36. I was not a good father to him. My daughter is doing well. She has three children of her own and is doing well. So I have failed in many ways."

Andy Griffith nearly died of a heart attack in 2000 and had a quadruple bypass on May 9. On October 16, 2002, he returned to Mount Airy for the highway dedication of the Andy Griffith Parkway, a ten-mile stretch of Highway 52.

During the visit he said, "I appreciate it. This is the biggest day of my life." He visited his cousins Lorraine and Earlie Gilley and his 91-year-old aunt, Verdi Cook, who made him a pumpkin pie. It was his first public visit to Mount Airy in forty-five years. Getting caught up in the emotion of the moment, he said, "He was a great father. He was a lot better man than me. I loved him, and I still miss him. He gave me my values and my sense of humor."

Two years later in 2004, he returned to Mount Airy for the dedication of Andy and Opie statue by TV Land during Mayberry Days on September 24. UNC-Chapel Hill recognized Griffith with a Lifetime Achievement Award in 2005. He donated many items to the Southern Historical Collection in September and on November 5, 2005, received the Presidential Medal of Freedom, the country's highest civilian award along with eighteen others including Carol Burnette, Paul Harvey, Jack Nicklaus and Frank Robinson.

For many years, Andy Griffith was active in politics and the Democratic Party supporting Governors Mike Easley and Beverly Perdue. Griffith gave his support for years especially in the 1984 Senate Campaign against conservative Jesse Helms to

Jim Hunt. Griffith even contemplated a run himself against Helms in 1990. In 2008, he supported Barack Obama and appeared in a hilarious video made by his former television son, Ron Howard, who appeared as Opie Taylor and Richie Cunningham from his role in the show *Happy Days.* In 2010, Griffith's political view backfired on his hometown, when he supported Obama Care appearing in a government made video.

Mondee Tilley of the *Mount Airy News* wrote, "The controversy was dubbed 'Mayberrygate' by media outlets after four Republican senators, including Sen. Richard Burr of Winston-Salem, objected to the commercial. The senators wrote a letter to Kathleen Sebelius, secretary of the U.S. Department of Health and Human Services, requesting that the department pull the ad and reimburse the government for any taxpayer dollars spent on the effort."

Betty Ann Collins, President of the Mount Airy Chamber of Commerce reported receiving communications from people cancelling travel plans to Mount Airy including one irate female potential visitor. "She did not agree with him doing a commercial like that and was disappointed in him for doing that and ended up holding Mount Airy, because we are home of Andy — holding us responsible to where she ended up canceling all of her reservations," said Collins.

Mount Airy probably wished Andy had practiced what he said in his comedy monologue "A Conversation With A Mule." "You knew politics wasn't going to help you out none and I am just learning."

In 2009, he reestablished his relationship with Grace Moravian Church with an "affirmation of faith." Reverend Tony Hayworth, his wife, and Emmett Forrest traveled to Manteo to meet with Griffith. The newspaper article in the Mount Airy News stated, "Membership in Grace Moravian Church could lead to Griffith's future interment in God's Acre, the church cemetery bordering North Main Street where graves are marked with simple flat stones in keeping with Moravian tradition." Andy Griffith's life and career had come full circle back to the church where his love of music was nurtured and the faith that was so important to him was reaffirmed.

He said once he would "work till I can't remember my lines anymore."Andy Griffith's last movie role came that same year in 2009's *Play The Game* playing Grandpa Joe, a widower who seeks love in a retirement home while learning from his grandson David how to become a lothario including a memorable sex scene with Edna played by Liz Sheridan. The film included both Ron Howard's brother and father, Clint and Rance.

In his last scene on camera, he is fishing with his grandson, David, played by Paul Campbell. He is most famous for walking to Myers Lake to fish with his son Opie Taylor and he ended his career with a grandson. Griffith's character says, "Life is good."

That same year Griffith joined Country Music Artist Brad Paisley in the latter's video for his song "Waiting on a Woman." The last scene shows Griffith sitting on the beach in a white suit. They filmed him walking off into the sunset, but did not use it. Andy is on a beach, wind blowing is his hair. Today, he rests on his farm near the beach with the wind from the ocean blowing over him. He is home in the soil of his beloved North Carolina.

A common scene in Mount Airy is seeing characters from the *The Andy Griffith Show* eating a pork chop sandwich in the Snappy Lunch even though Andy Griffith never tried one to the author's knowledge.

Six Mount Airy Police Officers arrested Otis Campbell at

3:15 p.m. on April 21, 2011. The town drunk was arrested on Main

Street, but not for public drunkenness in Mayberry. James Slate,

who portrays Otis Campbell, violated the 1963 downtown

sidewalk ordnance in Mount Airy. A crime wave in "Little

Chicago" as Mount Airy was once known. No, Slate aka "Otis"

stated it was for playing checkers in front of his son's store, the

Mayberry Country Store, which the Slates say was once a small

grocery store from which Andy Griffith delivered groceries. Slate

received repeated warning about obstructing the sidewalk before

he was carted off to jail in Dobson, paid a $500 bail bond, and was

released. He apparently did not have a key to the jail cell himself.

Slate claimed his constitutional rights were violated.

The story of Slate aka Otis's arrest went viral on YouTube

and with multiple news outlets and online sites. Nine months

passed with a continuance before a judge found Slate/Campbell

guilty and charged him $50. Slate/Campbell appealed to the

Superior Court stating the "ordinance is antiquated and detrimental to modern retail operations downtown."

So is Otis Campbell, a political prisoner, the victim of an overzealous police force or is it a whole bunch of fuss about nothing? Should we start a "Free Otis" campaign and contact Amnesty International? Only in Mayberry would this be a crime, but sadly, it was in Mount Airy.

The saga of Otis vs. The Man continued into July 2012 with Slate/Otis suing two police officers and the city over his arrest. The suit asks for $500,000 claiming loss of income and costs associated with the arrest. In the spring of 2013, a judge dismissed the when the district attorney agreed to drop charges if Slate dropped the civil suit ending the crime wave of Otis Campbell.

A year earlier, Betty Ann Lynn, then age 83, who played the character Thelma Lou, the girlfriend of Deputy Barney Fife, on *The Andy Griffith Show,* was the "victim of a robbery" in Mount Airy. Lynn lost $143 to an assailant, while shopping near a Lowes Food Store. Lynn moved to Mount Airy from Los Angeles in

January 2007 to get away from the urban landscape of crime and her West Hollywood home, which was broken into twice. She is often at the Andy Griffith Museum signing autographs and is one of the last survivors of *The Andy Griffith Show* and the last female, who had a recurring role. She once told the Mount Airy News "I don't deserve as much of the love as I get."

Born in Kansas City, Missouri, Elizabeth Ann Theresa Lynn was discovered on radio before Darryl F. Zanuck signed her to 20th Century Fox. Her first movie in 1948 film *Sitting Pretty* starred Robert Young. Next came *June Bride* with Bette Davis and more films. Her career on television began in 1953 on the ABC sitcom *Where's Raymond?* Lynn played Thelma Lou in Mayberry from 1961 until 1965. She made a final guest appearance in one episode during the sixth season (1965–1966) of *The Andy Griffith Show*.

In the 1980s, Barber Russell Hiatt, owner of the City Barber Shop decided to promote his business as Floyd's City Barbershop taking the title from *The Andy Griffith Show* and a cottage industry was born in Mount Airy, one that would keep the downtown area vibrant for decades to come.

Russell was friends with my father. Like many kids growing up, I got my haircut in the same chairs that tourists now flock to sit in and get their pictures made. My grandfather, Erie Perry, came from Tennessee to North Carolina to work in the textiles in the 1940s and by the 1960s, he enjoyed taking his oldest grandchild up to Main Street from his West Pine Street apartment he shared with my grandmother, Idell Bates Perry. Often these trips included a trip next door to the Snappy Lunch not for a porkchop sandwich, but for a ground steak sandwich or Andy Griffith's favorite, a hot dog.

In May 2012, I spied Emmett Forrest talking to Cecil Fulp, groundskeeper of the Gilmer Smith House, on Main Street in Mount Airy. I was not a good friend of Emmett Forrest, but I did enjoy talking to him whether on the Main Street or breaking bread with him in Barney's next door to our mutual friend Steve Talley's Frame Shop. Forrest always likes to talk Civil War and we decided whether he was or not that Nathan Bedford Forrest must be related to him. One of two men to go from private to Lieutenant General for the Confederacy in the War Between the States (Wade Hampton was the other.);

Emmett took it upon himself to collect Andy Griffith memorabilia and received many things from Andy himself. Most of his collection is on display in the Andy Griffith Museum on Rockford Street beside the Andy Griffith Playhouse.

Emmett Forrest, who was, another of those possibly named in *The Andy Griffith Show* as Emmett "The Fix It Man." Emmett has done his friend Andy and his hometown a great service in collecting and preserving this collection of memorabilia. He and Griffith had once pretended Lovill's Creek was the Mississippi River and they were Tom Sawyer and Huckleberry Finn. Mount Airy owes Forrest and all those who help keep the downtown vibrant a big thank you. All you have to do is visit nearby Stuart or Martinsville in Virginia to see what happens to a small town when the industry leaves and there is no tourism draw like Mount Airy. As Andy Griffith or Andy Taylor might say, "I appreciate it."

Many people have made Mount Airy home because of Mayberry and many businesses have sprung up accordingly. Julie Teague of Mayberry Consignments said it best in a recent issue of Our State. "Every small town in America would kill for what we have. The tourists come for Mayberry, but they fall in love with Mount Airy."

Tourism is big business in the "Granite City." In 2010, tourism brought 95 million dollars to Surry County. Among the Mayberry related businesses in town is Squad Car Tours, where visitors can ride around in a police car similar to those driven in *The Andy Griffith Show*. Among the drivers is Melvin Miles, who drives 1963 Ford Galaxie. Miles said of the show, "A lot of parents restrict television. *The Andy Griffith Show* is probably one of the only one of them that's fit to watch." In 2011, 58,000 visited Mount Airy and 305,000 since 2005.

Darrel and Debbie Miles grew up in southern Indiana as fans of *The Andy Griffith Show*. They are just one of the couples that came to Mount Airy because of Mayberry. Today, they operate Mayberry on Main. While watching an Andy Griffith

Show marathon on television they saw Goober Pyle (George Lindsey) advertising Mount Airy, North Carolina, and saw Mount Airy mentioned on *The Oprah Winfrey* show in 1986. Vacation trips to Mount Airy from southern Indiana began over the years. "It felt like heaven," Debbie says, "Mayberry people understand each other."

One day in April 2006, they decided to come to Mount Airy to look for a house. Darrell left his job of 36 years and moved to Mount Airy. They started a Mayberry Shop first across from Floyd's Barbershop and the Snappy Lunch in April 2006 and now in their present location Mayberry on Main at 192 North Main Street across from the intersection of Franklin and Main.

The Miles appreciate how good Mount Airy has it due to *The Andy Griffith Show.* They were naïve about the negative feelings towards Mayberry, but they "live in their own little Mayberry world" and they like the positive aspects of that. They even point out that in spite of what people think there were African-Americans in the early black and white episodes of the show and the later color episodes of the show late in the 1960s.

They point out that Andy never had a family reason to come back to Mount Airy as his parents were dead and he had no brothers or sisters. "Mount Airy owes that man a whole lot. He has touched our lives in great ways."

Darrel sells hot sauce along with the plethora of Mayberry items and antique reproduction signs. Their grandchildren Gregory, Gweneth, and Graiden live in Mount Airy along with their youngest daughter Samantha Miles. "Mayberry people are mostly good people" and so is the Miles Family.

Eleanor Powell of the Mount Airy News tells of another visit to Mount Airy by Andy Griffith. "…when his longtime friend, Emmett Forrest, lost his wife, Barbara, from a long illness. He and Cindi came to Mount Airy for the funeral at Grace Moravian Church in 2004. Departing from Mount Airy, the Griffiths passed by the Andy Griffith Playhouse and paused to look at the Andy Griffith statue that is erected near the front entrance. With a telephone call to Emmett, Andy jokingly let him know that a bird had laid droppings on his head. Being the friends that they were, Emmett got a bucket of water and washed the bird droppings from

Andy's statue." I believe it was Andy Griffith's last visit to his hometown.

Eleanor continued, "A friend has come and gone and we all have fond memories that we like to share. Some we keep to ourselves. Emmett said in a few words, 'He left a big footprint.'"

"Maybe Barney Fife said it best when talking about Sheriff Andy Taylor in Mayberry, but it applies to Andy Griffith and Mount Airy. "The people in this town ain't gotta better friend than Andy."

**Darrel and Debbie Miles having Mayberry fun in
Mount Airy including a visit with Betty Lynn aka Thelma Lou.**

The author's birthplace, the Northern Hospital of Surry County, just down the hill from the water tower that welcomes visitors and shows Andy and Opie headed to the fishing hole across Haymore Street from Andy Griffith's Homeplace.

153

The author's father, Erie M. Perry with his old friend Russell Hiatt in Floyd's City Barber Shop on August 29, 2012.

Andy Griffith with his parents, Carl and Geneva.

The train station then and now near the site of Andy
Griffith's birthplace.

Old Hollow "Stewarts Creek" Primitive Baptist Church is the final resting place of Andy Griffith's maternal grandparents.

White Plains Baptist Church is the final resting place of Andy Griffith's paternal grandparents and the Siamese Twins, Eng and Chang Bunker.

Graves of the Siamese Twins in White Plains.

Graves of John D. and Sallie E. Griffith in White Plains.

Marriage License

Virginia _Patrick County_ to-wit:

To Any Person Licensed to Celebrate Marriages:

You are hereby authorized to join together in the Holy State of M mony, according to the rites and ceremonies of your Church or relig denomination, and the laws of the Commonwealth of Virginia,

Carl Griffith and _Geneva Nu_

Given under my hand, as Clerk of _Circuit_ Court of _Patrick_ Co (or City) this ___ day of _Aug_, 19__

Marriage Certificate

To be annexed to the License, required by Section 5074 of the Code of Virginia, 1919, as amended by Act of February 16, 1910.

VIRGINIA: In the Clerk's Office of the _Circuit_ Court for the County (or City) of _Patr_

Date of Marriage _Aug ?? 1975_ Place of Marriage _Patrick Co_

FULL NAMES OF PARTIES _Carl Griffith_ and _Geneva Nunn_

Age of Husband _39_ years; Condition (single, widowed or divorced) _single_

Age of Wife _76_ years; Condition (single, widowed or divorced) _single_

Race (White or Colored) _white_

Husband's Place of Birth _Surry Co, NC_ (PRESENT) Mailing Address _Mt Airy N_

Wife's Place of Birth _Patrick Co Va_ Mailing Address _Mt Airy N_

Names of Husband _John D Griffith_ and _Sallie Griff_
Parents Wife _Sam Nunn_ and _Josina Nunn_

Occupation of Husband ___

Given under my hand this ___ day of _Aug_ 19__

Certificate of Time and Place of Marriage

I, _J S Ross_, a _Minister_ of _M E Ch_ Church, or religious order of that name, do certify that on the _22nd_ day of _Aug_, 19 at _Stuart_, Virginia, under authority of the above License, I joined together in the Holy Sta Matrimony the persons named and described therein. I qualified and gave bond according to law auth ing me to celebrate the rites of marriage in the County (or City) of _Patrick_, State of Virg

Given under my hand this _22nd_ day of _Aug_ 19__

(Person who certifies)

The Minister or other person celebrating a marriage is required, within thirty (30) days thereafter, to return the License and Certificate of th and his certificate of the time and place at which the marriage was celebrated to the Clerk who issued the License; failure to comply with these requirem the law makes the Minister or other person celebrating the marriage liable to a fine of not less than ten nor more than twenty dollars for each offen Section 5074 of the Code of Virginia, as amended by Act approved February 16, 1910, Acts 1919, chapter 28, pages 36 and 37).

Marriage Certificate of Carl and Geneva Nunn Griffith discovered by this author in the Patrick County Virginia Courthouse in Stuart, Virginia.

815

North Carolina State Board of Health
BUREAU OF VITAL STATISTICS

STANDARD CERTIFICATE OF BIRTH

1. PLACE OF BIRTH

County Surry   Registration District No. 86 2623   Certificate No. 111

Township Mt Airy   or Village

City   (No. 181 South   St: Ward)
(If birth occurred in hospital or institution, give its name instead of street and number)

2. FULL NAME OF CHILD   Andy Samuel Griffith   (If child is not yet named, make supplemental report, as directed)

3. Sex of child male   To be answered only in event of plural births.   4. Twin, triplet, or other   6. Parents married? Yes   7. Date of birth June 1, 1926 (Name of Month) (Day) (Year)

5. Number, in order of birth

8. FATHER	14. MOTHER
Full name Carl Lee Griffith	Full maiden name Geneva N. Nunn
9. Residence (Usual place of abode) If nonresident, give place and State Mt Airy	15. Residence (Usual place of abode) If nonresident, give place and State Mt Airy
10. Color or race White 11. Age at last birthday 30 (Years)	16. Color or race White 17. Age at last birthday 27 (Years)
12. Birthplace (city or place) (State or country) Surry	18. Birthplace (city or place) (State or country) Patrick Co Va
13. Occupation Nature of Industry Mechanic	19. Occupation Nature of Industry Housewife

20. Number of children of this mother (Taken as of time of birth of child herein certified and including this child.)   (a) Born alive and now living 1   (b) Born alive, but now dead   (c) Stillborn

21. Did you use drops in baby's eyes at birth to prevent blindness? Yes   If not, why not?

CERTIFICATE OF ATTENDING PHYSICIAN OR MIDWIFE*

22. I hereby certify that I attended the birth of this child, who was alive (Born alive or stillborn) at 3 (Hour a.m. or p.m.) on the date above stated.

23. (Signature) S. H. Worrell   (State whether physician or midwife)

24. P. O.

Given name added from supplemental report

25. Witness   (Signature of witness necessary only when 23 is signed by mark)

19   26. Filed July 5, 1926 27. J. C. Hill   Local Registrar

Registrar   28. P. O.

*When there was no attending physician or midwife, then the father, householder, etc., should make this return. If a child breathes even once, it must not be reported as stillborn. No report is desired of stillbirths before the fifth month of pregnancy.

Birth Certificate of Andy Samuel Griffith.

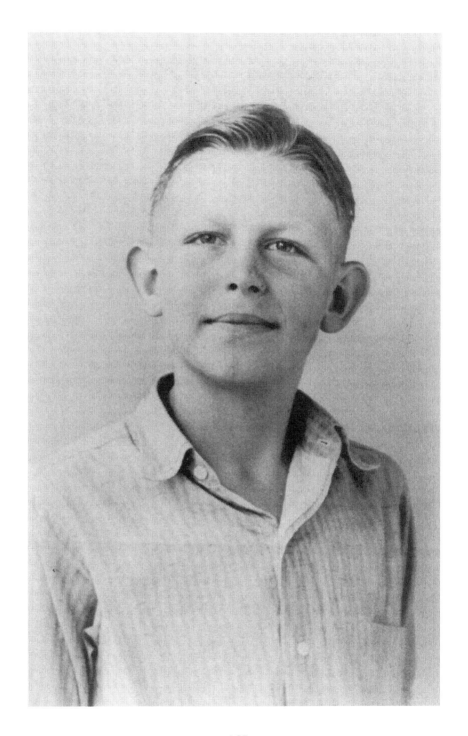

On the old farm-house ve-ran-da there sat Si-las and Mi-ran-da, thin-king of the

days gone by; Said he "Dea-rie don't be wea-ry, you were al-ways bright and

chee-ry But a tear, dear, dims your eye." Said she, they're tears of glad-ness, Si-las,

they're not tears of sad-ness; It is fif-ty years to-day since we were wed. "Then the

old man's dim eyes brigh-ten'd and his stern old heart it ligh-ten'd As he turned to

her and said:" Put on your old grey bon-net with the blue rib-bon

on it while I hitch old Dob-bin to the shay; Through the fields of

clo-ver on the way to Do-ver on our Gol-den Wed-ding Day.

Rockford Street School

**Andy Griffith, back row center, fourth from the left
wearing glasses.**

169

170

172

The Steele Building near the Old Well at UNC-Chapel Hill was the home to Andy Griffith while in college.

In *The Lost Colony* with first wife, Barbara.

The cast of Goldmasquers entered in the Carolina row: homas Slade, Jane Elliott, Ronnie Rose, Sa-
Drama Festival "In-Laws" is shown above short- ra Markham, K. D. Pyatt, and Gurney Collins.
ly before they left for Chapel Hill. Looking from Standing is Mr. Andrew Griffith.—News-Argus
left to right, they are: on the back row, David Photo.
John Smith, Phyllis Banks, Harold Kadis; front

Teaching at Goldsboro High School.

The house at 1208 East Mulberry Street, where Barbara and Andy Griffith lived while in Goldsboro, North Carolina.

The porch at 1208 East Mulberry reminded me of the porch on the Taylor House in Mayberry. Below, the Wayne County Museum in Goldsboro tells the history of the region.

With Patricia Neal in *A Face in the Crowd*.

Andy Griffith visiting Mount Airy High School production of South Pacific in 1966 including a kiss from Bettsee Smith McPhail.

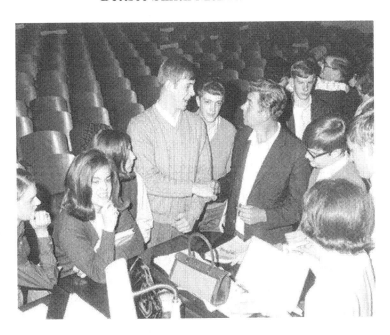

Below, Andy and Barbara with kids Andy "Sam" Griffith, Jr. and Dixie.

Hard to believe, but there was a time that Andy Griffith was the headliner and Elvis Presley was an opening act. Next page, yucking it up with "The King" on The *Steve Allen Show*. Below, Deacon Andy with Ed Sullivan.

183

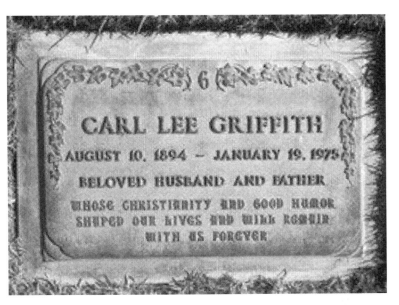

Nancy Stafford starred with Andy Griffith on *Matlock* and below with Melvin Miles on July 2012 visit to Mount Airy.

**Andy and wife, Cindi, during 2004 visit for dedication
of Andy Griffith Statue.**

188

SPECIAL SHOWING
Andy Griffith

In the new, critically acclaimed movie ...

"WAITRESS"

Showing at the Downtown Cinema
Admission Only $3 - Rated PG-13

SPECIAL DATES & SHOW TIMES

Friday, June 29 - 7:00 & 9:00 PM	Friday, July 6 - 7:00 & 9:00 PM
Saturday, June 30 - 7:00 & 9:00 PM	Saturday, July 7 - 7:00 & 9:00 PM
Sunday, July 1 - 2:00 & 7:00 PM	Sunday, July 8 - 2:00 & 7:00 PM
Monday, July 2 - 7:00 PM	Monday, July 9 - 7:00 PM
Wed., July 4 - 7:00 PM*	Wed., July 11 - 7:00 PM
*Out in time for fireworks!	

**Andy "Sam" Griffith Jr.'s grave at
Forest Lawn in Los Angeles.**

With daughter Dixie Nann Griffith in 2005 at the White House.

**The Andy Griffith Museum is on Carl Griffith Court at the
Surry Arts Council on Rockford Street.**

Emmett Forrest is shown above left with Mayor Jack Loftis and others opening the Andy Griffith Museum that is today beside the Surry Arts Council. Emmett, a long time friend of Andy Griffith, has spent years collecting materials, some from Griffith, those now make up the collection at the Andy Griffith Museum.

The author still sporting his long hair from cancer battle with Mayor Deborah Cochran above and Donna Fargo below on July 4, 2012.

"Andy is at peace and with God."

The day after Andy Griffith died was Donna Fargo Day in Mount Airy as the most famous female was coming home for several days to be Grand Marshal of the Fourth of July Parade. Coincidence or irony that the person who also has a highway named after her and was the songwriter and singer for several number one hit records in the 1970s was home the day after the death of the favorite son. I asked her that day if she ever met Andy Griffith. She remembered meeting George Lindsey aka Goober Pyle and she thought she met Andy, but our abbreviated conversation did not lend time to much thought for the "Happiest Girl in the Whole U. S. A."

Mayor Deborah Cochran proclaimed Donna Fargo Day saying, "This lady is beautiful inside and out…Today is a great day to celebrate for all of us as Donna Fargo has once again returned to her hometown." The favorite daughter showed why she is so beloved in her hometown. "Fargo told the crowd waiting for her autograph that while the day had a somber note due to the death of

Andy Griffith she was glad to be back home. 'We were all so sorry to hear about the passing of Andy. He will be missed by all of us.' Fargo said that Griffith, through his television career, changed America.' The show influenced our culture, and he personally showed us all how to be better people.'"

Earlier that morning, I rose early to get copies of the Mount Airy and Winston-Salem newspapers as I felt something might be of use to a historian, who was writing a book about Andy Griffith and Mount Airy. The town was eerily silent with only television crews out at the Andy Griffith Museum. There were several bouquets of flowers at the statue of Andy and Opie Taylor in front of the Andy Griffith Playhouse.

There was no secret burial crew digging at Grace Moravian Church and other than a neighbor and a rabbit, I saw virtually no one, but I felt the spirit of the town where I was born and it was strong. The parade was a great experience including many squad cars like the ones driven in *The Andy Griffith Show*.

Over two hundred years ago, a group of men declared their independence from the British Empire. I thought of the old car commercial that talked of baseball, hot dogs, apple pies, and Chevrolet. I thought of how engrained in the fabric of our nation this man from Mount Airy had become. Baseball, hot dogs, apple pie, and Andy Griffith might become a moniker for the town, as Andy loved hot dogs as he mentioned during his speeches dedicating the highway marker for him nearly a decade earlier and for anyone who ever watched *Matlock* knows that Andy often ate a hot dog. It goes back even to ""What It Was, Was Football"," where he famously mentions having a hot dog with a "Big Orange." He never had a pork chop sandwich at the Snappy Lunch as Charles Dowell invented that after Andy was long gone from Mount Airy. Readers will remember that Andy did make hot dogs at the Weiner Burger for his cousin Evin Moore.

At his last public appearance Griffith said, "I'm proud to be from the great state of North Carolina. I'm proud to be from Mount Airy. I think of you often, and I won't be such a stranger from here on out."

Griffith stated he would not be such a stranger when he came back for the highway dedication in 2002, but he was. I am not aware that he came back again except for the funeral of Emmett Forrest's wife and the TV Land statue dedication.

As I thought about it, I realized that he did not owe Mount Airy anything as he had done enough. Forrest might have said it best when I saw him on television several years ago stating Mount Airy had a four-letter tourism industry "A N DY." I am not sure Andy Griffith knew how people felt about him. I think Emmett Forrest might have summed it up best when he told his old friend Andy Griffith, "You don't have any idea how much people love you."

Of course, they loved the character Andy Taylor and not the real man as few of us knew him. There was one person who did know Andy Samuel Griffith, his wife, Cindi, who released the following statement on the day of his death.

"Andy was a person of incredibly strong Christian faith and was prepared for the day he would be called Home to his Lord. He is the love of my life, my constant companion, my partner, and my best friend. I cannot imagine life without Andy, but I take comfort and strength in God's Grace and in the knowledge that Andy is at peace and with God."

Griffith summed himself up this way seven years earlier. "I am just a 79 year old person. I worship, and I am kind of private…I have ups and downs like everybody but God through Jesus and prayer keeps me afloat. It fills me with joy. Even though sometimes you are not filled with joy. Sometimes you are down…I am a man like any other man. I have many failings."

Like all people, Andy Griffith was not perfect and he was not the characters he played. He was a very good actor and an award-winning musician as he started out to be at Grace Moravian Church. There is one thing that I can say about him. He brought happiness to many people all over the world and pride to his hometown. He is the only person from Mount Airy, North Carolina, to receive a Presidential Medal of Freedom and as Gomer Pyle might say, ""G-o-l-l-y"!

While writing this book, I watched everything I could find on DVD in which Andy Griffith starred. In 2007, he starred in *Waitress* with Keri Russell of the TV show *Felicity* and Nathan

Fillion aka Richard Castle from the ABC Show *Castle*. Griffith played a grumpy restaurant owner, who lived to eat Russell's character, Jenna's, pies. He said in one memorable scene that if everyone could just taste this pie it could change the world. While not apple pie, Andy Griffith changed the world and became ingrained in the American psyche as American as apple pie.

On July 4, 2012, I left the "Happiest Girl in the Whole U.S.A." and wandered up to the Andy Griffith Playhouse. There I found Patricia Comire and her fourteen-year-old son Benjamin, who had driven over from Martinsville after hearing of Andy Griffith's death. Known to me as "Pat Come Here" from our mutual friend Doug Stegall of Fieldale, Virginia, we began to talk about *The Andy Griffith Show*. Patricia, a schoolteacher and a "Helen Crump in search of her Andy," asked me questions about Mount Airy and Andy Griffith, which I replied, but it was Benjamin that impressed me. Benjamin showed me that day that there are young people who watch *The Andy Griffith Show* and that the "Love" Andy often talked about did endure.

Pat commented to me later about Mayberry and *The Andy Griffith Show*. "It has made me a little sad because I look at how things are now and wish so much that Benjamin could have those sweet simple days. Tradition and home raising seems to be a dying art. For me, tradition, respect and raising my child to love the Lord is natural. I just see how little of that is being installed in other children these days."

Way out on the prairie in Topeka, Kansas, my friend Deb Coalson Bisel, who grew up in Patrick County and is now a recognized Civil War Historian in Kansas told stories to the Topeka Capital Journal on July 3, "People kind of craved that sense of community and connection, and Mayberry represented that to people…One of the things that Andy Griffith did for me and for all people from North Carolina, is sort of the same thing that James Arness did for Kansas (Arness played Marshall Matt Dillon in Gunsmoke). There's an instant credibility and trust because of Andy Griffith. It's because he took that character to the world, and I'm forever in his debt for that."

201

A week later Nancy Stafford, who starred with Griffith on *Matlock* from 1986 until 1992 came to Mount Airy appearing at several locations including a tour with Melvin Miles of Squad Car Tours. In an article in the Winston-Salem Journal she said, "When I walked on that set the very first day, I was absolutely terrified. But he had a quick way of putting me completely at ease, and the whole set was welcoming…Andy was an amazing consummate professional. He expected a lot from the people around him because he gave that, and more."

The Mount Airy News commented on the favorite son after his passing. "Griffith also experienced his share of controversy. He was said to be, at times, cantankerous and difficult to work with. He most assuredly was able to hold a grudge, particularly against those he perceived as having wronged him or his family during his youthful days in Mount Airy. But even in those less-than-flattering parts of his life, Griffith has much to teach us. He could be difficult, but mostly because he demanded a level of excellence for which some weren't willing to work. He did hold grudges, but as he aged he became soft-hearted toward many of those who had, in fact, wronged him, and he showed the humility and wisdom to put aside those hard feelings and re-establish connections. Griffith also exhibited throughout his life an intense loyalty to his friends, whether those be from his childhood days or people he met along his climb to the top of his profession. He was quietly kind, often donating to charitable causes — many times he footed the bill for Christmas gifts for underprivileged families in the town of Manteo — and he worked hard to keep those donations private."

Griffith reportedly paid or worked to get internet/wifi on Roanoke Island. Back home in Mount Airy, he paid for the Mount Airy High School Band to go to Mardi Gras in New Orleans.

One aspect of the life and career of Andy Griffith that his mentor Reverend Mickey would approve is the many churches that use *The Andy Griffith Show* to illustrate Bible lessons including the book by Joey Fann *The Way Back to Mayberry: Lessons from a Simpler Time*. The Gateway Baptist Church in Tobaccoville has Bible study after watching an episode of *The Andy Griffith Show*.

Many people believe that the 'Mayberry Daze" will pass and that Mount Airy will forget about it. Maybe when all the baby boomers like me pass on, it will not be as popular. The simple life and ideas of living in the small southern town will go on and that is not a bad legacy to have or one Mount Airy should not promote and use to its betterment. Anything else would be as Gomer Pyle would say a "Shame, Shame, Shame!"

Writing this book has been strangely emotional for me whether it is fighting and beating cancer or just romanticizing one's hometown. Andy Griffith allowed me to get back in the saddle of my laptop and to take pride in the town where one was born is not a bad thing. The Right Honorable Mayor Deborah Cochran caught the right tone I think saying that Andy Taylor was "America's favorite father" and Andy Griffith was "Mount Airy's favorite son."

The marker in front of the Andy Griffith Playhouse states "Mount Airy to Manteo, a simpler time. a simpler place. a lesson, a laugh, a father and a son." This is the story of a father and a son whether it is Andy and Opie Taylor, Carl and Andy Griffith and for me and my father, who is synonymous with Mount Airy for me and to paraphrase Andy Griffith talking about Carl, a far better man than I am.

Mount Airy is like Paul Harvey said a place where "everybody knows everybody and everybody is worth knowing." In many ways, it is far superior to Mayberry and it will always be just home for me.

"I would like to continue to give people some small thing to make them laugh. What I would like to do, whenever I act or entertain, is to say some small truth. No preaching just to have some small thing to say that is true." Amen Deacon Andy Griffith. Amen!

Patricia Comire and son, Benjamin, on July 4, 2012.

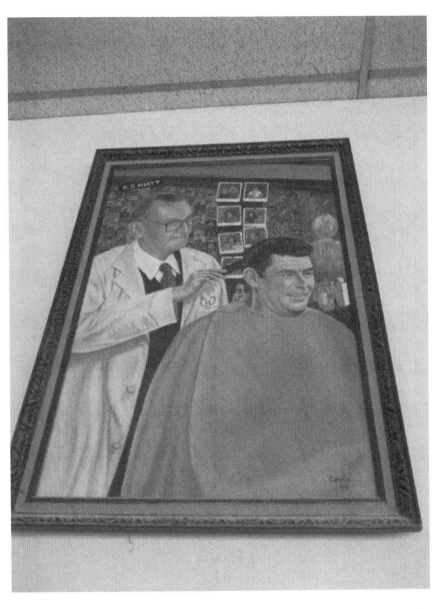

A fictional painting of Russell Hiatt cutting Andy Taylor's hair

July 4, 2012

July 3, 2013   From Mount Airy to Manteo to Mayberry

Clergyman Henry Ward Beecher, brother of Harriet

Beecher Stowe, the woman Abraham Lincoln recognized as

starting the Civil War with her novel *Uncle Tom's Cabin* once said,

"Mirth is God's medicine. Everybody ought to bathe in it." It is

true that laughter is the best medicine.

This book has brought me much laughter and much success

in the short time since it premiered at Mayberry Days at Mayberry

on Main in Mount Airy, North Carolina, in September 2012.

Beyond Mayberry: A Memoir of Andy Griffith and Mount Airy

North Carolina was featured as part of the national book festival

The Virginia Festival of the Book sponsored by the Virginia

Humanities Foundation on March 20, 2013, in Charlottesville,

Virginia. I was part of a panel titled "What We Write, Why We

Write" at the Northside Library at 300 Albemarle Square in

Charlottesville, Virginia.

"The mission of the Virginia Festival of the Book is to

bring together writers and readers and to promote and celebrate books, reading, literacy, and literary culture. As the largest gathering of authors, writers, and readers in the Commonwealth, and, indeed, the Mid-Atlantic region, the Book Festival has become an integral part of the community and is presented in a unique partnership of contributors that includes the VFH, foundations, corporations, bookstores, schools, libraries, area businesses and organizations, and committed individuals. This partnership results in programs in a wide range of topics set among a variety of venues throughout the City of Charlottesville, County of Albemarle, and the University of Virginia.

Along with the staff, almost every aspect of the Festival is organized and generated by Festival Committees consisting of community volunteers who generously contribute their time and energy. Programs range from traditional author readings and book signings to a StoryFest day of children's authors and storybook characters; from a panel on how to publish a novel to a discussion on running a book club; from a workshop on bookbinding to a discussion on freelancer's rights. All programs are open to the public; with the exception of a few ticketed events, programs are free of charge."

Other were not enamored with the book. I had one clerk at one of the many places I sell this book tell me, "My granddaddy went to school with Andy Griffith and said he was a jerk. I watch the show, but when they had to pay Andy to come back to dedicate that highway and that statue that says a lot about how he really felt about Mount Airy."

If you grew up anywhere near Mount Airy, North Carolina, you could not escape Andy Griffith. If you grew up as a baby boomer watching television, you could not escape Andy Griffith. Most people have an opinion about him, love him or hate him, but you cannot deny that he is part of our lives.

He is also part of our economy. Just drive down Main Street in Mount Airy and there is hardly an empty storefront. Contrast that with Martinsville about an hour away that does not have the tourist draw that is "A N DY" as Emmett Forrest, Andy's boyhood friend and the man who collected most of the material in the Andy Griffith Museum in Mount Airy, liked to say.

At Christmas 2011, I was diagnosed with prostate cancer and had surgery on February 15, 2012. Dealing with the cancer, thoughts of mortality, the physical condition it causes for a man such as bladder control and erectile dysfunction, leads to depression and I fought that. I needed something to bring me out of the dark and get me writing again. I struggled with history projects that usually I dive into, but then one day I ran into Emmett Forrest on Main Street. He too was fighting illness, bladder cancer, I believe, and he said to me after inquired about his health that it was "like jumping off a ten story building. Someone asks you about the seventh floor of the fall how you are doing." Emmett answered, "Well, so far the ride has been pretty good." I marveled at his positive attitude and as I always did, I asked him if he had spoken to "Mr. Griffith" lately. I never called him Andy because I did not know him. Emmett told me about their conversation. A month or so later Andy Griffith died on July 3, 2012.

The library in Shawsville, Virginia, made this poster for a book signing I did about Beyond Mayberry: A Memoir of Andy Griffith and Mount Airy North Carolina.

I had written and toyed with the idea of writing about Andy Griffith, but I did not want to write about The Andy Griffith Show (TAGS). I wanted to write about Andy Griffith and Mount Airy, North Carolina, where we were both born. In fact, I was born about a month after TAGS premiered on CBS just down the street from the house Andy grew up.

I began to explore the common experiences and the different Mount Airys we both knew. I began to watch episodes. I began to watch movies Andy Griffith starred in thanks to Netflix. I was surprised at how good a dramatic actor he was. I went to Goldsboro and found the house he and his first wife, Barbara, lived in along with the high school he taught music. I found his dorm at UNC-Chapel Hill and read some of his papers in the Wilson Library. I went through huge files at the Mount Airy Museum of Regional History and I read many articles online with interviews.

I began to write. I found my voice again. I think the reason was that I was laughing so much at the man from Mount Airy. If there is anything funnier in television history than the TAGS when

Don Knotts and Jim Nabors were on it, I have never seen it. I have always thought that after Knotts left Andy Griffith seemed bored. He was bored and eventually left for other challenges. He struggled as I was when I started this book, but he preserved and he left us some of the best comedy on the small screen.

I have a book that is written as things happened with his death and the day after July 4, 2012, when Donna Fargo came to town to be Grand Marshall for the parade. There is no more professional and classy woman that I have ever met. When introduced at the museum, she talked about Andy. Before she had asked me how I was feeling, as she knew I was sick. She has MS, but she will not leave until everyone that wants to see her or get her autograph gets there time with the "Happiest Girl in the Whole USA."

I usually write about things long after they happen, but this was an opportunity to catch Mount Airy on the day it lost the most famous son and the day after when the most famous daughter came home. I walked over to the statue of Andy and Opie headed to the fishing hole and found Patricia Comire and her teenage son, Benjamin. She says her family calls her a "Helen looking for an Andy," but she likes Ernest T. Bass, so she likes a man on the edge too. People often talk about the "Mayberry Thing" dying away, but Benjamin reminded me that day there are many in the younger generation that still love TAGS. He knew all about it and talked and talked.

I think many times that there is much envy and jealousy aimed at Andy, but to wish for the "Mayberry Thing" to go away is to wish for Mount Airy's downtown to lose the economic prosperity it now enjoys and I am against that way of thinking. You might be against the silliness or the greed that it engenders, but do not forget that Andy Griffith gave many of us pure joy in the laughter and entertainment he produced over six decades from standup comedy to Broadway to movies to television to musical recordings, the only thing he ever received awards.

This book is part biography of the man and part memoir of the town we both knew as youths. If you are looking for negative stories about him, there are not many because no one would go on record and hearsay does not interest me. What I found was a man who did not suffer fools and who was very serious about his craft. He never left Mount Airy. He took with him, shared it with the world and he put it on the map. There is only one person from Mount Airy, North Carolina, to have a Presidential Medal of Freedom and we should be proud of him.

Andy Griffith was not Andy Taylor. I think his father Carl Griffith was Andy Taylor. Described as "the funniest man I ever met" by Andy's first wife, Carl Griffith was the inspiration for his son. This book is also a little about my father, who grew up the son of mill workers in Mount Airy. In 1966, Erie Perry and Andy Griffith found themselves in line together at the Hospital Pharmacy just a block from Andy's parent's home and across the street from where I was born. When I asked my father what he said to Andy, he said nothing because he was so shocked to see him. When I asked my father what Andy said to him like Mark Twain my father, who tells the ladies he is still "Erie-sistible" said Andy was so shocked to see him, he didn't say anything either. Such is life living in the town that produced two legends in their own time.

John Peters of the Mount Airy News wrote an opinion piece titled *One of my favorite authors passed his latest book to me the other day*. Peters wrote, "It was none other than local historian Tom Perry, and his latest book is "Beyond Mayberry: A Memoir of Andy Griffith and Mount Airy, N.C."

"His books sometimes have a bit of a folksy feel to them. Rather than reading like an academic work, or one by a writer trying to impress us with his vast literary capability, reading Perry's books gives me the feel of someone chatting with me on the street, telling me a story. I wish more writers could figure out how to do this.

A hallmark of Perry's work, at least the ones I've seen, is a healthy dose of photos. "Beyond Mayberry" is no exception, and this may be its strongest appeal. Don't get me wrong, I enjoy reading through the chapters — I am, after all, a writer at heart more than anything else — but the pictures he includes bring his subjects to life in ways that are difficult to accomplish with words.

I'll give you a couple of examples from his more recent effort. On page 157 there is a picture of Andy Griffith from his childhood days. I don't know exactly what year, but I'd guess Griffith was somewhere between the ages of 7 and 11 when that one was shot.

It could have been a school picture, or perhaps one his parents had done of their only son. Looking at that photograph I don't see a famous actor or musician. Instead, I see a small boy, a ghost of a smile on his face — or maybe it's an expression of longing for something his parents cannot afford to give him. Then again, he could be thinking of what he's going to do that afternoon after the photographer is done and he's free to run off with his friends.

I've seen that sort of expression in my own kids, and looking at that photo in the light of comparing it to my own children, I can personalize some of Griffith's life — compare some of his struggles and joys to those of my kids, or my own. And with that simple photo, Perry made the entire book more alive for me, as a reader.

That's why I enjoy local writers such as Perry. The good ones understand how to connect with their local audience, how to bring area history alive for their readers, and I think he's done that again with his latest book."

Jo Maeder wrote a piece about the book for the Greensboro News & Record Published 12-23-2012. Here is that conversation.

Q: You've edited or published 35 books on regional history. This is your first that's part memoir, part biography with former Mt. Airy resident Andy Griffith as the subject. What were the challenges and rewards in writing this kind of a book?

This book had been on my mind for a long time since I found the marriage certificate of Andy's parents in the Patrick County Virginia courthouse. When he passed in July, I escalated my efforts. I was recovering from prostate cancer surgery and I used the laughter of the Andy Griffith Show to get me going again. This book was easy to write as I grew up near Mount Airy and like most people my age Andy was part of my life from as long as I could remember. The reception of this book has been amazing from people telling me how they feel about it to the amazing sales it is generating.

Q. *Beyond Mayberry* is loaded with details such as Andy Griffith had a birthmark on the back of his head his mother called "Andy's strawberry patch." He swept out buildings for $6 a week to buy his first trombone. You also delve into his parents and grandparents past. You pored over old records in libraries and courthouses. How did you keep it organized and was there a lot you didn't use?

Most of this book was from printed sources. The Mount Airy Museum of Regional History had a huge archive of files about Andy Griffith and Mount Airy. I did visit Andy's papers at UNC-Chapel Hill and Goldsboro, where he lived and taught school after graduating college. Almost everything I found is in the book with the focus being mainly on Mount Airy.

Q: You say Andy Griffith never said for sure that Mayberry was based on Mt. Airy. His cagey reply when asked was, "It sure sounds like it, doesn't it?" There's been a bit of controversy over where the "real" Mayberry is located. Could you describe it and your thoughts on the subject.

In Jerry Bledsoe's book about biking the Blue Ridge Parkway, he tells about visiting the Mayberry Trading Post and Addie Wood the owner telling about Andy visiting the place as a kid. In Andy's papers at UNC-Chapel Hill, he had a photocopy of the related pages and the paragraph I mentioned above was circled without comment. You can read into that maybe that Andy was pleased to see that. I think his visits to Mayberry Virginia were a pleasant memory of his youth with his mother's family from Patrick County, where his mother, Geneva Nunn Griffith was from, but that is just my opinion.

Q: The photographs in the book are fantastic. Is there somewhere on the internet where they, and those not used, can be viewed? Which are your favorites?

Most of the photos came from people who knew Andy, Mount Airy Museum of Regional History, and the Mount Airy News. I loved the cover photo of Andy with his parents in the parade in Mount Airy on his 31st birthday, which I believe was for the opening of his movie *A Face in the Crowd.*

Q: What do you think are the biggest misconceptions about Andy Griffith?

I think many people assume that Andy Griffith was Sheriff Andy Taylor. He was not. I came to believe that Andy Taylor was Carl Griffith, Andy's father, who was a great storyteller and Andy's first wife said was "the funniest man I ever knew" and she was married to Andy Griffith. Andy Griffith was a serious actor and he was playing a role. In real life, he was not as approachable as the character he played.

Q: Why do you think the appeal of *The Andy Griffith Show* has endured through generations?

I think the Andy Griffith Show was one of the funniest shows ever on television especially when Don Knotts was on it. I think Andy took Mount Airy with him into the show and that made it real. I think part of the appeal of the show is that it is taken from real life.

Q: You wrote this book while recovering from surgery for prostate cancer that has side effects that, though generally temporary, could throw any man into a depression. How did writing the book help you through that time?

I had surgery in February 2012 and when Andy Griffith died in July, I was struggling to start work again. As I said earlier, I used the laughter from the show to heal, but it was a subject that I knew and that made it easier to write about something so close to home for myself too. Prostate cancer for men is not easy, but I had robotic surgery at Baptist in Winston-Salem and am now almost fully functional again.

Q: What were the most unexpected discoveries you made about yourself and Andy Griffith while writing or promoting *Beyond Mayberry*?

I think the thing about Andy that I did not realize was how much a product of his parents he became. He got his musical ability from his mother's side, which was the only thing he ever received recognition such as Grammy Awards for his albums. He got his story telling from his father Carl and probably the acting.

As for myself, I think I was surprised at how much pride I began to feel for being from the same place as Andy Griffith. He received a Medal of Freedom from President George W. Bush and if you look at the ceremony, you can see the joy Andy Griffith in his face. It is the first thing in the book because I don't think we will see anyone from Mount Airy getting one of those any time soon and I came to feel what a memorable event that was for Andy Griffith and Mount Airy.

As the year progressed with my recovery and the incredible success of this book, I came to feel enormous pride in Andy Griffith and the town he and I were both born. At the many events I attended selling this book I heard many memorable quotes. Here are a few of them. "It says something about a show that is still on fifty-three years after it premiered." At a flea market in Southwest Virginia a fellow said to me, "The best thing about getting old and getting Alzheimer's is you get to see a new episode of the TAGS every day."

From Mount Airy, North Carolina, to Westminster, South Carolina, I encountered many people who were "Tribute Artist."

These people's love of the TAGS sends them out all over the country impersonating characters from the show. Some fine folks they are from Tom Rusk, who works with the Mayberry Festival in Westminster and could be a great Barney Fife with his squad car. There is Allen Newsome, who is the only Floyd The Barber I have encountered, who does a Podcasts that is the highlight for many who love TAGS. I sat in Westminster and watched David Browning do the "Mayberry Deputy" for fifteen minutes and I laughed the entire time. Christie McLendon was portrays "Andylina" was enormously helpful throughout my first year of "Andy." She is beautiful inside and out along with possessing some serious chops as a performer herself. Kenneth Junkin, a very sober Otis, was a great help to me. I made many friends among these people shown on the following pages.

One day in early spring, I found myself in Manteo, North Carolina, and on my way back from Fort Raleigh, where the first attempt of the English failed resulting in The Lost Colony, the play Andy Griffith appeared in and introduced via video for many years. Just down the street from the historical site and outdoor theater, I found myself in front of a locked gate with a fence that screamed "Stay Out." It was Andy Griffith's home in Manteo and one assumes his final resting place. I did not attempt to sneak in to get a photo of his grave and risk jail time, but I did pause at the entrance and marveled at the journey from Mount Airy to Manteo he took in his eight plus years and the journey he and this book about him has taken me over the last year.

Having a year to reflect on this book and Andy Griffith's contribution to this country and most importantly his hometown I am reminded repeatedly about Andy's cousin Evin Moore, who operated the Weinerburger that Andy did not leave Mount Airy he took it with him. He did that he took it beyond Mount Airy and beyond Mayberry. He took his hometown to the world and he made many people happy. As I said, "Laughter is the best medicine."

David L Browning, Michael Oliver, Jeff Branch, Phil Fox,
Mike McLendon, Alma Venable, Sandy Pettigrew, Kenneth
Junkin, Allan Newsome and Angie English Brown in
Westminster, South Carolina in 2013.

I had a memorable weekend in Westminster, where Maggie Peterson, "Charlene Darling" sat beside me most of the day on Saturday. She still sings "Salty Dog" and was a joy to talk too.

With David Browning "The Mayberry Deputy" at
Westminster, South Carolina.

The man, the town, the legend

Andy Griffith admirer travels down memory lane

By Jo Maxwell

Greensboro News and Record December 23, 2012

BOOKS

Griffith

Continued from Page H1

Sequels

Continued from Page H1

"Beyond Mayberry" contains many photographs, including this one of barber Russell Hiatt in front of his Mount Airy barber shop. In the 1960s, Hiatt decided to promote his shop as Floyd's City Barber Shop, taking the title from "The Andy Griffith Show," that also launched the cottage industry that Mount Airy enjoys to this day, according to author Thomas Perry.

The first copy of Beyond Mayberry sold in Mayberry on Main in Mount Airy with owner Darrell Miles on the right. Still the only place to get an autographed copy of Beyond Mayberry in the "Real Mayberry." Below, my cousins Robert and Madison Pennington from Georgia.

Cousin Adam Pennington reenacting Andy and Opie going fishing with his son, Adam.

Beginning in June 2013 I began my new career as a Darrel Miles Tribute Artist continuing in the tradition of the many people who come to Mount Airy for Mayberry Days every September. Darrel and Debbie own Mayberry on Main, which was where we brought this book out in September 2012.

Selected Bibliography

Patrick County Deed Book 30 page 509
Patrick County Marriage Register Volume 5 page 27
Patrick County Land Book 1925
Patrick County Historic Society
      Nunn Family File

Books

Claiborne, Jack and Price, William, editors. *Discovering North Carolina: A Tar Heel Reader.*

Collins, Terry. *Andy Griffith: An Illustrated Biography*, Mount Airy, 1995.

Smith, O. Norris. *The Nunns of 18th Century Virginia*. Greensboro NC.

Articles

American Profile: October 1, 2005.

Readers Digest
      "He Never Left Home"

Our State: Down Home in North Carolina.
      October 2005, Volume 71, Number 5
      Andy Says "Hey" page 32
      Festival of Color page 116
      Mayberry Bound page 120
      July 2012, Volume 80, Number 2
      Mayberry page 86

Wachovia Moravian, February 1968, Vol.78 No.2
      "The Andy Griffith I Knew" by Edward T. Mickey, Jr.

Newspapers

Cleveland This Week April 16, 1967

Denver Post July 6, 2012, "Andy Griffith's Denver Based Daughter"

The Enterprise April 23, 2005, article by Fred Gilley

Mount Airy News

"Griffiths Say Goodbye To Friendly City Today," April 1966
"Andy Griffith Praised As Only Man To Ever Add Whole Town NC—Mayberry," October 13, 1978
"Music Was One Of Griffith's First Loves," March 29, 1992
"Andy says it was a thrill visiting his boyhood home," March 27, 2003
"Churches using Andy Griffith Show...," December 18, 2005
"Two cancel travel plans due to ad by Andy Griffith," June 2010
"Andy Griffith rebuilds ties with church," July 2009
"Lessons Andy Griffith could teach to all of us by," July 2012
"Andy Griffith left imprint on 'Mayberry' residents," July 4, 2012
"Andy's relationship with hometown was tragic," July 5, 2012
"Otis Files Lawsuit Against Police, City," July12, 2012
Other dates: June 26, 1993; October 23, 2002; September 24, 2004;

Mount Airy Times

"Andy Griffith Given Going Away Party," July 21, 1944
"City Plans Huge Andy Day," May 31, 1957
Other dates: July 15, 1947; January 28, 1949; September 16, 1949; July 30, 1961;

Topeka Capital Journal,

"Topekan from 'Mayberry' celebrates Griffith," July 3, 2012

Winston-Salem Journal

"After Setbacks, Griffith Finds Deep Happiness," November 10, 1984
"Andy Is Mighty Proud To Return To Mayberry," April 12, 1986
"Memory: Cousin Recalls Andy Griffith's Boyhood," September 1990
"The Pride of Mount Airy," July 4, 2012

The Wachovia Moravian

"The Andy Griffith I Know." February 1968

Video

Andy Griffith: Hollywood's Homespun Hero, 1997.
North Carolina People with William Friday, December1993.

About Thomas D. Perry

J. E. B. Stuart's biographer Emory Thomas describes Tom Perry as "a fine and generous gentleman who grew up near Laurel Hill, where Stuart grew up, has founded J. E. B. Stuart Birthplace, and attracted considerable interest in the preservation of Laurel Hill. He has started a symposium series about aspects of Stuart's life to sustain interest in Stuart beyond Ararat, Virginia." Perry holds a BA in History from Virginia Tech in 1983.

Perry started the J. E. B. Stuart Birthplace Preservation Trust, Inc. in 1990. The non-profit organization preserved 75 acres of the Stuart property including the house site where James Ewell Brown Stuart was born on February 6, 1833. Perry wrote the original eight interpretive signs about Laurel Hill's history along with the Virginia Civil War Trails sign and the new Virginia Historical Highway Marker in 2002. He spent many years researching traveling all over the nation to find Stuart materials including two trips across the Mississippi River to visit nearly every place "Jeb" Stuart served in the United States Army (1854-1861). Tom can be seen on Virginia Public Television's Forgotten Battlefields: The Civil War in Southwest Virginia with his mentor noted Civil War Historian Dr. James I. Robertson, Jr. Perry has begun a collection of papers relating to Stuart and Patrick County history in the Special Collections Department of the Carol M. Newman Library at Virginia Tech under the auspices of the Virginia Center For Civil War Studies.

In 2004, Perry began the Free State Of Patrick Internet History Group, which has become the largest historical organization in the area with over 500 members. It covers Patrick County Virginia and regional history. Tom produces a monthly email newsletter about regional history entitled Notes From The

Free State of Patrick that goes from his website www. freestateofpatrick.com.

Historian Thomas D. Perry is the author and publisher of over twenty books on regional history in Virginia surrounding his home county of Patrick. A Virginia Tech graduate, he studied under renowned Civil War Historian James I. "Bud" Robertson, and speaks all over the region and country. Perry's collection of papers, books, and images are housed in the Special Collection Department of the Carol M. Newman Library at Virginia Tech.

In 2009, Perry used his book Images of America Henry County Virginia to raise over $25,000 for the Bassett Historical Center, "The Best Little Library in Virginia," and as editor of the Henry County Heritage Book raised another $30,000. Perry was responsible for over $200,000 of the $800,000 raised to expand the regional history library.

He is the recipient of the John E. Divine Award from the Civil War Education Association, the Hester Jackson Award from the Surry County Civil War Round Table, and the Best Article Award from the Society of North Carolina Historians for his article on Stoneman's Raid in 2008. In 2010, he received acknowledgement from the Bassett Public Library Association for his work to expand the Bassett Historical Center and was named Henry County Virginia Man of the Year by www. myhenrycounty.com. Perry also recently received the National Society of the Daughters of the American Revolution Community Service Award from the Patrick Henry Daughters of the American Revolution.

Historian Tom Perry at the site he saved, J. E. B. Stuart's Birthplace, the Laurel Hill Farm, just outside Mount Airy in Patrick County, Virginia.

Charles A. Brintle, my old Civil War Buff buddy from Yadkin County, North Carolina, holding a proof of this book told me the story of his maternal grandfather Floyd A. Kidd, who worked at the Mount Airy Furniture Factory, of buying a coke from Andy Griffith selling from a wooden tray in the same factory Carl Griffith worked for his years.

Acknowledgements

Thanks to Charles A. Brintle, Patricia and Benjamin Comire, Charles and Mary Agnes Dowell, Emmett Forrest, Jennifer Gregory, Debbie Hall, Russell Hiatt, R. Wayne Jones, and Darrel and Debbie Miles. Special thanks to Amy E. Snyder for getting me started and seeing me through my illness.

Special thanks to Ace Snyder and Jack Riekehof-Snyder.

Photo Credits
Photos courtesy of the Surry County Historical Society Minick Collection. Mayberry on Main, Wayne Jones, Mount Airy News, Winston-Salem Journal, Denver Post, and author's personal collection. No images from Viacom, Emmett Forrest or the Surry Arts Council were used in this book.

R. Wayne Jones of Aiken, South Carolina, shared stories of his mother a student of Andy Griffith at Goldsboro in Wayne County imagine that. Here Wayne is reading a book by this author about himself in Pigeon Forge, Tennessee, as he portrays my boyhood hero J. E. B. Stuart all over the country.

Index

A

A Face in the Crowd, 9, 63, 80, 81, 82, 179
Ainslie Pryor, 75
Albert McKnight, 49
Alma Venable, 84, 108
Andy Griffith Homeplace, 130, 153
Andy Griffith Parkway, 22, 108, 137
Andy Griffith Playhouse, 38, 46, 49, 93, 95, 101, 106, 134, 147, 150, 196, 200, 204
Ararat, Virginia, 239
Audie Murphy, 85
Aunt Bee, 84, 96, 108, 112, 131

B

Bannertown, 101, 111
Barbara Bray Edwards, 43, 73, 74, 75, 76, 82, 84, 134, 150, 175, 177, 182
Barber, 128
Bettsee Smith McPhail, 88, 181
Betty Ann Collins, 139
Betty Lynn, 68
Birth of the Blues, 58
Blu Vue, 112
Blue Bird Dinner, 129
Blue Ridge Elementary School, 14
Blue Ridge Parkway, 22, 29, 33, 34, 68
Bob Smith, 19
Brintle, 242, 243
Briscoe Darling, 123
Brown, 239
Bunker, 37, 40, 159

C

Cape Fear and Yadkin Valley Railroad, 35
Carl Griffith, 4, 19, 31, 34, 39, 43, 46, 51, 69, 87, 88, 100, 104, 131, 134, 155, 162, 192, 204, 242
Chapel Hill, 63, 69, 70, 71, 73, 76, 77, 134, 138, 173
Charles Dowell, 95, 97, 197
Childress, 30, 33, 40
Cindi Griffith, 95, 135, 150, 187, 198
Civil War, 2
Clint Britton, 73
Cook, 138

D

Deb Coalson Bisel, 201
Deborah Cochran, 194, 195, 204
Dixie, 182, 191
Don Knotts, 14, 88, 91
Donna Fargo, 194, 195
Douglass Benison, 51

E

Earle Theater, 81, 104
Ed Sullivan, 8, 78, 183
Edwards, 73
Eleanor Donahue, 104
Eleanor Powell, 65, 82, 134, 150
Elia Kazan, 79, 80
Elvis Presley, 78, 183
Emmett Forrest, 51, 55, 101, 140, 146, 147, 150, 191, 198, 243
Evin Moore, 43, 65, 80, 86, 131, 197

F

Fancy Gap, 112, 114
Fife, 127, 129
Floyd Pike, 55
Floyd's City Barber Shop, 21, 128,
    145, 149
Frances Bavier, 108

G

Garnett Steele, 51,52
Geneva Nunn Griffith, 4, 15, 19,
    31, 39, 40, 41, 43, 51, 84, 108,
    131, 155, 162
George Lindsey, 149, 195
George W. Bush, 9
Gilley, 110, 138, 237
Gilmer Smith House, 146
Goldsboro, 73, 74, 176, 177, 178,
    244
Gomer Ledge, 78
Gomer Pyle, 14, 20, 79, 106, 133,
    199, 204
Grace Moravian, 16, 18, 57, 58, 62,
    63, 98, 140, 150, 196, 199
Graves, 16, 18, 83, 160, 161
Griffith, 127, 128, 193
Guillain-Barre Syndrome, 135

H

Hal Cooke, 77
Haymore Baptist, 16, 17, 54, 55, 62
Henry County, 2
Hill., 239
Hillsville, 114
Hudson Graham, 22
 Huggins, Vic 77
Hutchens Cleaners, 106

J

J. E. B. Stuart, 2
J. E. B. Stuart Birthplace, 2
J. S. Rodgers, 31
James Kingsbury, 51
James Slate, 143
Jerry Bledsoe, 34
Jimmy Stewart, 85
John and Scenna Phillips, 31
John D. and Sallie E. Griffith, 161

K

Katherine Warren, 74
Kathleen Sebelius, 139
Ken Berry, 88
Keri Russell, 199
Kibler Valley,, 32
Knotts, 127

L

Laurel Hill (Birthplace of J. E. B.
    Stuart), 239
Lee Kinard, 78
Leonard Rosengarten, 136
Lester, 2
Loftis, 193
Lynn, 68, 144, 152

M

Main Street, 127, 128
Manteo, 63, 72, 73, 85, 87, 135,
    140, 203, 204
Mark Twain, 21
Martinsville, 2
Mary Jophina (Jopina or Jossina or
    "Jo Pinney") Cassell Nunn, 31
Matlock, 8, 9, 135, 136, 186, 197,
    202

Maurice Evans, 79
Mayberry, 68, 128
Mayberry Days, 21, 138
Mayberry on Main, 11, 108, 143, 148, 243
Mayberry Presbyterian Church, 68
Mayberry Trading Post, 29, 33, 34
Melvin Miles, 118, 148, 186, 202
Methodist Church, 52, 125, 135
Mickey, 57, 58, 59, 60, 61, 62, 63, 64, 98, 203, 237
Miles, 148, 149, 150, 152, 243
Minick, 243
Moody, 106
Mount Airy, 35, 36
Mount Airy Furniture Factory, 43, 100, 242
Mount Airy High School, 65, 66, 67, 99, 181, 203
Mount Airy News, 65, 81, 82, 96, 134, 139, 140, 145, 150, 202, 238, 243
Mount Airy Times, 87, 238
Mount Airy, North Carolina, 2
Mount Pilot, 109, 110

N

Nancy Stafford, 186, 202
No Time For Sergeants, 79, 82, 85, 88
North Carolina Granite Corporation, 123
Northern Hospital of Surry County, 15, 19, 153

O

Onionhead., 85
Oprah Winfrey, 149
Orville Campbell, 77

P

Patricia Comire, 200, 206
Patricia Neal, 179
Patrick County, 2, 11, 15, 29, 31, 32, 33, 34, 37, 43, 68, 162, 201, 237, 239, 241
Paul Harvey, 138, 205
Paul Young, 72
Perry, 2, 3, 5, 6, 19, 146, 239, 240, 241
Peter Cassell, 31
Pilot Mountain, 19, 109, 110
Pork Chop Sandwich, 96, 128
Put On Your Old Gray Bonnet, 50

R

R. Wayne Jones, 243, 244
Raleigh Little Theater, 75
Renfro Corporation, 66
Richard Linke, 85
Richard O. Linke, 77
Roanoke Island, 13, 18, 72, 84, 203
Robert Merritt, 66
Robertson, 239
Rockford Street School, 38, 46, 49, 88, 95, 134, 168
Ron Howard, 139, 141
Russell Hiatt, 10, 145, 207, 243

S

Sam and Mary Jophina Cassell Nunn, 31
Sam Dobyns, 17
Sam Nunn, 32, 34
Samuel Walter Nunn, 32
Scales, 32, 38
Siamese Twins, 37, 40, 159, 160

Simmons, 40
Snappy Lunch, 21, 55, 91, 95, 97, 128, 142, 146, 197
Squad Car Tours, 118, 148, 202
Steele Dorm, 70
Steve Allen, 85, 183
Steve Talley, 146
Stuart, 20, 31, 32, 37, 147, 162, 239, 241, 244
Stuart, James Ewell Brown "Jeb", 239
Surry Arts Council, 95, 104, 192, 193, 243
Surry County Historical Society, 36, 243

T

Taylor, 15, 18, 20, 22, 39, 40, 50, 52, 55, 86, 95, 96, 99, 102, 104, 106, 112, 129, 131, 133, 139, 141, 147, 151, 178, 196, 198, 204, 207
Tharrington, 5
The Andy Griffith Show, 8, 9, 13, 14, 34, 52, 68, 86, 89, 91, 95, 100, 104, 106, 109, 142, 144, 145, 147, 148, 149, 196, 200, 201, 203

The Lost Colony, 72, 73, 85, 135, 175
Thelma Lou, 68, 104, 144, 152
Toast, 111

U

University of North Carolina, 69

V

Virginia Tech, 21, 239, 240

W

W. A. "Red" Underwood, 76
Waitress, 199
Wally's, 118
Weiner Burger, 65, 131, 197
"What It Was, Was Football", 77, 197
William Martin Griffith, 40
William Morris Agency, 78, 136
Worrell, 38

Y

Yeatts, 68

Related Websites

Laurel Hill Publishing LLC www.freestateofpatrickcom

Mount Airy Visitors Center www.visitmayberry.com

Surry Arts Council http://www.surryarts.org

Mount Airy Museum of Regional History
www.northcarolinamuseum.org

Surry County Tourism www.verysurry.com

Squad Car Tours www.tourmayberry.com

Snappy Lunch www.thesnappylunch.com

Mayberry on Main www.facebook.com/notifications#!/mayberryonmain

Main Oak Emporium www.mainoakemporium.com

Wally' Service www.wallysservicestation.com

North Carolina Granite Corporation www.ncgranite.com

Talley's Custom Frame Shop www.facebook.com/pages/Talleys-
Custom-Frame-Gallery/185955838100107

Scenic Gifts www.scenicgiftsmtairy.com

Made in the USA
San Bernardino, CA
31 July 2016